The Church Transforming

Advance Praise for *The Church Transforming*

"Every once in a while, a book comes along that changes the terms of a long, stale argument and shows us the way to better, deeper, more vital questions. *The Church Transforming* is just such a book. Michael Jinkins says the Reformed faith is not so much an embattled tradition that needs either to be fiercely protected and defended or, on the other hand, casually abandoned. No—it is a vital project to be pursued. And that project is precisely the ongoing endeavor of 'recovering the Christian faith as God's calling of humanity to new life in Jesus Christ.' Figuring out how to do that faithfully and well in our time and circumstances is a wondrous and compelling vocation—worthy of our best energy, imagination, and thought. Jinkins provides abundant wisdom for the journey."
—Craig Dykstra, Senior Vice President, Religion, Lilly Endowment, and author of *Growing in the Life of Faith*

"For me and other younger Reformed Christians, Michael Jinkins's *The Church Transforming: What's Next for the Reformed Project?* is a breath of fresh air. Long unsatisfied to be merely defenders of Reformation era perspectives, we have been seeking a voice of wisdom that might help us orient our work as we seek to follow Christ into new and different contexts. By encouraging Christians to rediscover the innovative power of a thinking faith that intentionally engages wonder and diversity, Jinkins is clearly emerging as that voice."
—Landon Whitsitt, author of *Open Source Church: Making Room for the Wisdom of All* and blogger at landonwhitsitt.com

"Michael Jinkins examines the common clichés about Reformed faith—including charges that it is incurably contentious, doctrinaire, and spiritually cold—and turns them inside out, showing how much creativity and hope the Reformed project has to offer a fractured culture and suffering world. Leaders of churches in the Reformed tradition can take heart from this book and, along the way, enjoy Jinkins's lively and engaging style."
—Barbara G. Wheeler, Director, Center for the Study of Theological Education, Auburn Theological Seminary

The Church Transforming

What's Next for the Reformed Project?

MICHAEL JINKINS

EDITED AND WITH AN INTRODUCTION BY
SUSAN R. GARRETT

WJK WESTMINSTER
JOHN KNOX PRESS
LOUISVILLE · KENTUCKY

First edition
Published by Westminster John Knox Press
Louisville, Kentucky

12 13 14 15 16 17 18 19 20 21—10 9 8 7 6 5 4 3 2 1

Book design by Sharon Adams
Cover design by Night & Day Design
Interior photo credit: Erich Lessing / Art Resource, NY

Library of Congress Cataloging-in-Publication Data

Jinkins, Michael
    The church transforming : what's next for the Reformed project? / Michael Jinkins with Susan Garrett.
        p. cm.
    Includes bibliographical references (p.   ).
    ISBN 978-0-664-23843-8 (alk. paper)
    1. Church renewal—Presbyterian Church (U.S.A.) 2. Church renewal—Reformed Church. 3. Presbyterian Church (U.S.A.)—Doctrines. 4. Reformed Church—Doctrines. I. Garrett, Susan R., 1958- II. Title.
    BX8969.5.J56 2012
    285'.137—dc23

                                                                          2011051975

Contents

Acknowledgments

The ideas in this book have taken shape over the past several years as I have spoken in a variety of church and academic settings. Although these essays and addresses focused on a single theme, they were in need of a firm editorial hand to bring them all together into a coherent book. I am grateful to Dr. Susan R. Garrett, dean and professor of New Testament at Louisville Presbyterian Theological Seminary, for serving as editor and for writing her superb introductory chapter. I also thank David Dobson at Westminster John Knox Press for agreeing to publish the book.

This book had its genesis in the inaugural Lupberger Lecture series at St. Charles Avenue Presbyterian Church in New Orleans, Louisiana, where I delivered what would eventually become the first two chapters. I wish to thank Ed Lupberger for his vision in establishing this lecture series, which is designed to bring current scholarly thinking to a general audience. I also wish to thank the senior pastor, Don Frampton, and the session and congregation of the St. Charles Avenue Church for their extraordinary hospitality. I also delivered portions of these two chapters as the Jones Lectures at Austin Presbyterian Theological Seminary in 2011. I am grateful to President Ted Wardlaw for his invitation to do so. From the time I first gave the lectures in New Orleans, I hoped they might form the core of a larger published project that could serve as a reminder for Reformed Christians of the distinctive character and creative power of our historic movement.

The chapter on worship and wonder began as a convocation address I delivered at Austin Presbyterian Theological Seminary, where I was dean and professor of pastoral theology for a number of years. A version of the address was subsequently revised into a scholarly article for publication in the *Journal of Religious Leadership*. Though the present chapter is very different from that article, I am grateful to the editors of the journal for permission to use the essay as the core from which I crafted the chapter.

The chapter on schism was presented at Princeton Theological Seminary in spring 2009 as part of the Calvin Conference organized to celebrate the five hundredth anniversary of John Calvin's birth. This presentation was subsequently published in *Theology Today*. That summer a more popular version of this essay was presented at Montreat Conference Center in conjunction with its observance of the Calvin anniversary. I would like to thank the editors of *Theology Today* for their permission to use some portions of the published version of this chapter.

I am grateful to Susan Diluca, administrative assistant in the president's office, for the significant work she did on this manuscript and to Dana Cormack, executive administrative coordinator for the president, for the innumerable ways she supported me in the work that made this book possible. I also thank Elana Levy, who helped with proofreading the manuscript.

I am grateful to my wife, Deborah, for her patience. During our time in Scotland in the summer of 2010, I spent part of each day sequestered in the cottage kitchen—my makeshift study—writing. And in the summer of 2011 as we vacationed at our home on Saint Simons Island, Georgia, she graciously endured the same writing schedule. This has been our pattern for several years, wherever we have spent our summers. And while it certainly works for me, I recognize that it does require a considerable sacrifice on her part. I am grateful that she supports my vocation as a writer and that she has done so through more than thirty-five years of marriage.

Finally, I thank Dr. Pamela G. Kidd, chair of the Board of Trustees of Louisville Presbyterian Theological Seminary, and the entire board for their support both of me as president and of the role my writing plays in this vocation. I am grateful to my colleagues at Louisville Seminary for their devotion to our common mission, and to our students—the next generation of leaders for the church.

The Isenheim altarpiece, by Mathias Gruenewald

Introduction

Bold and Biblical—A Vision for the Reformed Project

A Crucial Moment for the Reformed Project

Today Reformed identity is up for grabs. Recent defections and threats of schism in some Reformed denominations[1] have been triggered especially by the debate over homosexuality, but that debate manifests broader underlying issues pertaining to the interpretation of Scripture and tradition. In *The Church Transforming: What's Next for the Reformed Project?* Michael Jinkins argues that being a Reformed Christian means not so much that one espouses certain doctrines or shares a particular interpretation of the Bible but that one has committed oneself to being involved in a certain kind of project: the project of renewing the faith according to the Word of God. Jinkins explores the nature of this project especially as it is presently unfolding in the Presbyterian Church (U.S.A.)—though there is much here that is relevant for other denominations in the Reformed family.

The title of this book is intended to point to the church *as always in the process of being transformed*, and also to remind us that the church is itself *called to be an agent of transformation in the world*. The title deliberately echoes the phrase "the church reformed, always to be reformed (according to the Word of God)," which has been a watchword for Reformed churches since the sixteenth and seventeenth centuries.[2] The historic motto reflects a conviction that humans' best efforts are affected by sin, including our efforts to proclaim our Christian beliefs and to order church life; therefore the church *always* stands in need of reformation, renewal, and change.

The motto also reflects the conviction that our living and sovereign God is never constrained by our doctrine, or even by our time- and culture-bound interpretations of the written words of Scripture. God is free to speak and act in new ways in our changing world—yet, these self-revelations will be consistent with God's ways and means as revealed in the person of the incarnate Word, Jesus Christ. Christ was sent to transform our relationships to God and to one another through the power of the Holy Spirit working in and among us (see 2 Cor. 3:17–18).

To begin to discern "what's next for the Reformed project," we have to pay close attention to the context in which we find ourselves. At least three major challenges face the Reformed churches at this moment. First is the pervasive and seemingly intractable conflict over the interpretation of the Bible; second is disagreement over how best to respect the authority of classic Reformed theologians and confessional tradition; and third is Reformed church members' uncertainty about what to think and how to act in our changing social and cultural context, in which human and religious diversity of many sorts press upon us. I will briefly address each of these challenges— challenges that may instead be viewed as opportunities, as Jinkins demonstrates.

Battles over the interpretation of the Bible are nothing new in the Reformed churches, which participated in the widespread social and ecclesiastical upheaval over the theory of evolution early in the twentieth century.[3] In the PC(USA), creation versus evolution is not the controversial issue it once was, though it remains sharply divisive in some other Reformed denominations. But opposing interpretive stances that emerged in the evolution debate have developed into comprehensive worldviews that underlie other controversies in the Reformed churches today. One's position on any of the hot-button issues often correlates with one's views on other such issues, and reflects a distinct set of answers to questions about how we know what we know and how we make sense of the Bible: How do spoken and written words convey meaning, and how do readers appropriate that meaning? What is the relationship between the Bible and reason? What part of the biblical message (if any) is constant and what changes based on our social and cultural location? These contrasting worldviews in turn serve as the basis for elaborate judgments and divisions, not only in the church but also in the social and political arenas. The Reformed project, if it is to thrive, will have to address this situation of conflict over the Bible.

A second problem facing the Reformed churches pertains to how we best uphold and value the authority of the Reformed tradition. Shirley C. Guthrie discussed this issue in terms of *the double crisis of identity and relevance*.[4] In some churches so much value is placed on identity (adherence to tradition, often interpreted as propositional truths) that the church becomes exclusive and judgmental of all who differ. New information or perspectives are discounted in attempts to safeguard doctrine, polity, or practice. At the other extreme, in their quest for relevance some churches jettison tradition and historical memory altogether, losing their identity in the process.

Both approaches to tradition are problematic. On the one hand, insisting on adherence to tradition understood as propositional truths can lead not only to exclusion of those whose interpretations differ but also to suppression of imaginative and critical thinking. As Jinkins argues, a church too tightly wedded to a narrow construal of traditional doctrine or practice excludes critical thought and is unable to respond creatively and effectively to rapidly changing circumstances. On the other hand, using the resources of history, tradition, liturgy, and theology in a merely superficial way (or not at all) renders churches vulnerable to cultural forces that promote idolatry. The church that has lost its memory is in a state akin to senility and prone to repeat the mistakes of the past.

Jinkins insists that the aim of the Reformed project is not to pass on and enforce adherence to a particular, narrow understanding of the Bible or the confessional tradition but to renew our passion for living as members of the body of Christ—albeit in certain characteristic ways. "The purpose of the Christian faith, from a Reformed perspective, is not to make us more religious but to make us human, like Jesus" (see p. 22 below). Much as our forefathers and foremothers in the faith did, we strive to worship and serve God, honoring the Bible and the confessions, yet remaining open to the Spirit that reforms and transforms us in accordance with God's revelation in Jesus Christ.[5]

A third problem facing the Reformed churches is a social and cultural context that has changed drastically over the past half-century.

If the church is to be both relevant and faithful, it cannot simply go on conducting business as usual in this post-Christian, multicultural, multiracial, multireligious, cyber-connected world. An authentic Reformed response to social and cultural difference requires humility to see the world as others see it, acknowledgment of the intelligence and integrity of those who hold their convictions as deeply as we hold our own, and genuine interest in ways of life and thought that may not be naturally comfortable for us. Addressed to other Christians, such an openhearted response reflects a Reformed conviction that our unity depends not on us (or on our "right" doctrine) but on what God has done for us in Christ. Addressed to non-Christians, such generosity reflects a Reformed conviction that we are called to love the *whole* world, and not just those who are like us. As Miroslav Volf writes, "The reach of God's love is the scope of our respect."[6]

By no means does our stance of respect toward others exclude evangelism, for there are many today who are open to hearing the Gospel: "'The harvest is plentiful, but the laborers are few; therefore ask the Lord of the harvest to send out laborers into the harvest'" (Luke 10:2). Jinkins argues that today's changed social landscape requires nothing less than a "missional vision" analogous to the one that shaped Christian thinking in the United States generations ago when Reformed men and women had the courage and the confidence to move west, building seminaries to provide ministers for churches that did not yet exist in communities that had barely begun to form. Surely the gospel is as true now as it was back then: God still works through Jesus Christ to seek and to save, to liberate, and to raise the dead to new life. Adventurousness and confidence are all that we lack. May the Holy Spirit grant those dispositions to us!

The essays in this volume address the interrelated problems or factors described above by presenting anew the case for constructive critical engagement with the Bible and with Reformed history and theology. In considering how best to draw on these precious resources, Jinkins rejects what Brian Blount has called "the dominant paleontological perspective" on interpretation. According to that perspective, "meaning is like a fossil, or to bring it closer to home, like a bone that a dog buries in the back yard." Given the right tool, any interpreter can dig up the bone and hold it up for the world to see and affirm, "That's a bone!"[7] The problems with this interpretive model are many, but above all it cannot account for the persistence of differences in our interpretations—differences evident when we compare the readings of even our wisest interpreters. Rather than envisioning tradition as a plot of land to be excavated, Jinkins suggests that the Bible and the Reformed legacy are like vast, rich fields to be stewarded, sowed, tended, and harvested, season after season. Christian communities work together to reap the bountiful produce of these fields—produce suitable to nourish the faithful in vastly different times, places, and cultures.

In their use of the resources handed down to us, Jinkins insists, Reformed Christians must practice what he calls a "thinking faith." Our faith is a thinking faith when we reflect on history and tradition deeply and appreciatively, yet also critically. Our faith is a thinking faith when we are not afraid to question established opinion; to explore the best that secular knowledge has to offer; to identify and challenge idolatry, superstition, and hypocrisy; to engage with genuine interest and respect even those with whom we disagree. Only a thinking faith can meet the complex challenges facing the church today.

Reformed Interpretation of Scripture

Given the recent divisive controversies in Reformed denominations, it seems evident that biblical interpretation is one area in desperate need of such open-minded and critical analysis. The Bible is more relevant now than ever, and people are hungry to "hear what the Spirit is saying to the churches" (Rev. 2:7). But this climate of hunger and need has encouraged ways of reading Scripture that oversimplify it and dilute or distort its teachings. So, before I turn to a preview of the essays in this volume, I will offer brief reflections on Reformed interpretation of the Bible in our present context.

The interpretive approach I advocate parallels the one that Michael Jinkins delineates for interpreting our broader Reformed theological and confessional heritage. I suggest that we respect Scripture without becoming locked into a narrow, literalist reading of it, and that we strive always to discern how the Spirit is leading us to appropriate and apply biblical wisdom in our own cultural contexts. I argue that we need to cultivate *a hermeneutic of generous listening* and to recapture a vision of ourselves as a *bold and biblical people*. In all these ways, I believe, we can build bridges that span our divides and enhance and strengthen our evangelism.

Reformed Interpretive Principles and Their Limitations

John Calvin famously compared Scripture to a pair of spectacles that bring God's revelation into focus: "So Scripture, gathering up the otherwise confused knowledge of God in our minds, having dispersed our dullness, clearly shows us the true God."[8] Calvin, himself a humanist scholar and an expert on the ancient Latin philosopher Seneca, recognized the need for learned interpretation of Scripture. As Cornelius Plantinga writes, "Calvin fed on knowledge as gladly as a deer on sweet corn."[9] When it comes to biblical interpretation, Calvin recognized, learning is necessary because the Bible is an ancient text written in foreign languages. Moreover, it is not only clergy who need knowledge to be wise interpreters. Calvin and other Reformers wanted to ensure and facilitate the education of all believers, so that all members of the church would be skilled students of Scripture.[10]

The guidelines for Reformed interpretation of the Bible as it developed through the centuries have been spelled out elsewhere. Shirley Guthrie, for example, identified eight such rules, which can all be supported from the confessional tradition and observed in the work of Calvin and subsequent Reformed interpreters. Paraphrased, the rules as identified by Guthrie are

1. We trust the Holy Spirit to enliven the Word and make it a Word to us.
2. We read any given passage of Scripture with openness to hearing the whole of Scripture as it may bear on that topic.
3. We read Scripture in light of God's self-revelation in Jesus Christ, which shows us God's character and God's will for our lives.
4. We always keep sight of the one commandment of God that summarizes all other commandments, namely, love for God and for all our neighbors.
5. We trust our conversation partners in the church (both those who are living and those who are dead) to guide and correct us.

6. We respect Scripture's demand for attention to the ancient languages, history, and cultures in which the Bible took shape.
7. In reading Scripture, we seek not to restore the church of yesterday, but to live into God's vision for our own time and place.
8. We read Scripture as ones who are fully cognizant of our limitations and fallibility, and who are therefore open to changing our minds and being corrected. [11]

All of these presuppositions and commitments shape our biblical reading and our theology and, in the PC(USA), the way we educate seminary students. In this connection, rule 6 is especially significant: candidates for ordination must take an exam in biblical exegesis that demonstrates their ability to work with the biblical languages and to analyze the historical, literary, and linguistic contexts of Scripture. These skills are central to *historical criticism*, a loosely conjoined set of strategies for reading biblical texts in their original historical contexts that took hold during the eighteenth century as a product of the Enlightenment.

Enlightenment thinkers aimed to make reason the sure foundation for knowledge and insisted on applying the same standards of evidence and proof to study of the Bible as were used in secular historical analysis. When historical criticism first rose to prominence, many presumed that it would establish a foundation for interpretive agreement. This hope persisted through the modernist era and still predominates in seminaries and divinity schools today. Across the theological spectrum, many theological educators and their students continue to insist that looking at texts in their literary, historical, and sociocultural contexts provides control on our natural human tendency to read into the text what we want to see there and thus permits "correct" interpretation of the biblical texts. [12]

I myself teach historical-critical methods because I believe that they can contribute substantially to enriched understandings of Scripture, but I find that these methods do not bring interpretive agreement. None of us is wholly objective; we all bring a complicated array of knowledge, experience, critical faculties, and imaginative sensibilities to the reading task. I once taught a brilliant graduate student who came from a sectarian tradition with a distinctive interpretation of Paul. I noticed that this student's exegesis of Pauline texts was always perfectly defensible according to historical-critical criteria—yet always consistent with his own strong theological position. *How does he do that?* I marveled time and again. The answer is, *we all do that.*

Use of historical-critical methods can actually accentuate disagreement among interpreters. One reason for this unintended consequence is that historical-critical analysis reveals both the complexity of the biblical writings and the variety of perspectives reflected in them. In addressing any given question, historical critics must make a whole series of analytical judgments, so that there are not one but many points at which they can and do diverge. Another reason why historical analysis can exacerbate interpretive disagreement is that practitioners of historical criticism have different ideas about what the Bible is and hence different ideas of what their interpretive goals should be. Where does meaning reside? In the historical events to which the texts refer? In the mind of a given author? In the minds of the first flesh-and-blood audience or readership? These are only a few of the ways historical critics have construed the object of their inquiry. Different definitions of the task at hand lead to different outcomes.

So, while historical criticism contributes greatly to our understanding of the biblical texts, it has not minimized disagreements but emphasized them. We ought to be doing better at letting seminarians and church people in on that secret and teaching them to become not merely *learned* interpreters of Scripture but *thinking* interpreters of Scripture. Learned interpreters stand in Calvin's own tradition, but there are plenty of learned interpreters who refuse to let themselves or anyone else really think, because they are afraid that the thinking will lead people to stray outside the bounds of orthodoxy. Several academic institutions in the Reformed tradition have recently fired tenured professors or board members for openness to scientific views, especially evolution.[13] These incidents represent a tragic departure from the Reformed tradition, insofar as they confuse adherence to narrowly construed doctrine with genuine faith and effectively deny the Reformed doctrine of the sovereignty and freedom of God. If God is genuinely sovereign over all creation, then we may pursue scientific inquiry wherever it may lead, trusting that ultimately it will lead us back to God. As my colleague Gene March likes to say, God is big enough to take all our questions; God isn't going to break.

Interpretive Differences and Real-World Interpretation

Luke Timothy Johnson observes that we heirs of the Enlightenment have routinely assumed that something has to be historical in order to be true.[14] That view has become so pervasive in the culture and in our theological institutions that it seems like common sense; thus, the historical-critical method has risen to its current status as the way to show what the text "really" means. The inerrantists on the one hand and the participants in the Jesus Seminar on the other hand or the creationists on our right and the evolutionists on our left disagree on whether human reason or written revelation takes priority in historical analysis, but they all agree that what matters is what really happened.

Historical inquiry is not the only way of knowing reality, however. As Johnson argues, there are also moral, aesthetic, and experiential ways of knowing reality, which historical methods for analysis can never capture. When we are open to these other ways of knowing, we find that the tradition is far richer and more informative than we suspected. Carol Zaleski discovered this richness, for example, in her work on ancient and modern near-death experiences.[15] If one insists that the only important question is whether the near-death experience "really happened," one cuts off debate even before it starts. First, it is not clear what would count as evidence for historicity in regard to such events. Second, the perception and reasoning of skeptics on the one hand and true believers on the other hand are so profoundly controlled by each side's own presuppositions that neither is likely ever to be converted to the other point of view. But if the researcher asks, rather, *what do such experiences mean within the cultural context of those who report them*, then the accounts unfold like opulent tapestries, full of texture, beauty, and meaning. Asking this question of biblical texts yields similar beauty and wealth of meaning, as do appropriations of the text through art and music.

Exaggerated confidence in the historical-critical method also discourages attention to the connections between our reading strategies and our respective positions on the various theological, political, and social issues that divide us. We can become so focused on the elusive original meaning or authorial intention of the biblical texts that we fail to teach students how to discern and evaluate how the biblical texts are deployed in the real world. In our seminary Bible courses we too often take students back to the preexilic period, or the postexilic period, or the period of Second Temple Judaism—but we do not give them sufficient guidance on how to understand what our texts mean for millions of flesh-and-blood readers *today*. Our students become experts at BibleWorks software, but they cannot make heads or tails of the way some Dispensationalists use the Bible to justify the geographic expansion of Israel. They can pass the Presbyterian ordination exam in biblical exegesis, but they cannot explain to you how their own exegetical approach differs from that of Joel Osteen or T. D. Jakes, who reach more people on a given Sunday than the vast majority of PC(USA) pastors will reach in a lifetime. They can defend their own particular view on abortion, be they pro-life or pro-choice, but they cannot tell you how and why the opposing point of view makes perfect sense to millions of people. Until we educate our students and church members in real-world biblical interpretation, we will not be educating them well.

There are, to be sure, educators and activists who are convinced that it is wrong to discuss a view they consider mistaken and dangerous or to accord it attentiveness or respect. According to this way of thinking, opposing views are best mentioned with scorn and derision or else not mentioned at all. But how will our students serve effectively if they have been taught to shun the discourse and worldview of all whose beliefs differ from their own? How will they make their way through the contentious social, political, and organizational circumstances that they will surely encounter in their work if they can only speak their native tongue? What hope of peace and cooperation do we have for our world if we dismiss all who differ from us as irrational and foolish, as heretics, or even as terrorists? We do not have to believe what others believe—but we ought to try to *understand* one another's beliefs, for our mutual benefit.

Focusing on real-world interpretation shifts our interpretive goal from finding the final or ultimate meaning of the text to discovering how and why different interpreters read the way they do.[16] We should be helping people to become more self-aware as interpreters and to adopt a hermeneutic of generous listening toward Christians with whom they disagree. Generous listeners assume that their opponents in debate are probably not raving lunatics. They may

even be quite rational and comprehensible if one grants their prem-
ises and understands their interpretive strategies. In his pioneering
ethnographic work among the Azande, anthropologist E. E. Evans-
Pritchard famously noted that the Azande's so-called witchcraft
made sense if you understood its underlying assumptions and the
types of questions it was believed to answer. I once taught a course
on New Testament views on evil, suffering, and death to a class that
included a student from Madagascar. He was continually amazed by
the fact that our class could discuss this topic and *not* assume sorcery
and demonic possession as givens. By the end of the course he was
not persuaded of our views or we of his, but we all learned a lot.
We did not come to agreement, but we grew in understanding. Such
growth is a chief goal of real-world interpretation.

I suggest that the topic of homosexuality and the Bible illustrates
the potential fruitfulness of instruction in real-world interpretation.
Parties on both (or all) sides of the homosexuality debate regularly
invoke the Bible, but to very different ends. If we examine the literature and discourse of this debate, we can see how people's prior
assumptions affect their interpretation—both their assumptions about
the topic in question and their more general interpretive assumptions
about the nature of the Bible and how to use it to provide warrant for
ethical arguments.[17] When I have taught this topic, I have encouraged
students to take a more detached view than they may be accustomed
to doing. Their task for the exercise is not to defend one position or
the other, but to act as a commentator on the debate itself and to try
to understand the inner workings of both sides of the argument.

Doing so involves a number of steps: determining who is involved
in the debate and what is at stake for all parties; identifying biblical texts regularly invoked as evidence in the debate; determining
how each party actually makes sense of the texts in question (observing, for example, how much attention they pay to literary and historical context and whether they insist on interpreting passages in
light of other, overarching biblical motifs); determining what other,
peripheral texts or pieces of nonbiblical evidence are brought into
the discussion; and finally, applying the same kinds of interpretive
questions to students' own belief system. What kind of document
do they themselves understand the Bible to be? To what extent do
they understand its teachings (on homosexuality or any other issue)

to have been conditioned by biblical cultures, and does that make any difference in how they apply them to the present? Should specific teachings trump broader principles, or vice versa? What roles do nonbiblical traditions, human reason, or human experience play in how they work out their own beliefs?[18]

Close examination of scriptural interpretation around moral issues such as homosexuality is a frightening endeavor for many, because entire worldviews are often at stake. But the freedom we have as a consequence of God's freedom for and from the world[19] means that we can hear other people's views without damaging or disgracing either God or ourselves. In one lesson in an introductory seminary course, colleague Carol Cook and I presented a number of short scenarios in which ministers needed to respond to situations involving lesbian, gay, bisexual, or transgendered people. For example, in one scenario a group of concerned parents requests to meet with you as minister to persuade you to speak to the school board about their objection to the formation of an LGBT coalition chapter in their children's high school. We challenged the students to respond to each scenario from two perspectives: from the viewpoint of an ally of LGBT people, and from the viewpoint of someone who opposes same-sex relationships. Caricatures of either view were ruled out of bounds; students had to use actual interpretive strategies typically employed by the various parties to the current debate.

This assignment was a hard task for everyone, no matter his or her prior stance on the issue. Yet it was a successful exercise. One of our students said, "Give me my arm and my leg back—I've never been stretched this far!" But she was joyful. She had trusted in Christ to hold her secure even as she strived to imagine herself into what was to her an unaccustomed point of view. She emerged with her own faith deepened and transformed.

As Reformed Christians we need not be threatened by interpretations of Scripture different from our own, for we trust in our sovereign God's freedom to speak to each one in the language and culture that the person will understand. In turn, we recognize ourselves as free to listen generously to others, seeking to understand their point of view empathetically. Such generous listening does not preclude disagreement or critique of others' views but ensures that we will engage rather than talk past one another. We have to hear their analysis and their evidence and genuinely try to understand. Jesus commanded us to love our enemies. I am appealing for something more basic: that we listen to one another, remembering that we are not enemies at all, but brothers and sisters in Christ.

Some minds *might* change as a consequence of our generous listening, but conversion is not the goal. The goals, rather, are to enlarge our mutual understanding and strengthen our commitment to loving and living with one another in Christ, and to become more observant and reflective about what we are actually doing whenever we interpret biblical texts. The payoff is greater clarity on where we ourselves stand on any number of spiritual, ethical, and social issues, and improved ability to engage others in meaningful, productive, respectful discussion. We observe how the Bible is interpreted in the real world, cultivate new habits of attentiveness and critical reflection, and engage those with whom we disagree in a way that helps us to identify common ends and work cooperatively for Christ. Thus we live out the conviction that Scripture is not an end in itself, not an object of worship, but a vehicle through which the Spirit speaks in witness to the living God, transforming us to be more like Christ. It is not Scripture but the risen Christ who is the center and measure of any authentic Christian faith.

Bold and Biblical

Luke Timothy Johnson contends that "we need to recover and embrace a scriptural imagination, to imagine the world as Scripture imagines it, not looking for proof texts, not trying to do an archaeological dig, but trying to recover the sense of Scripture as a living city in which we are citizens and whose language we know and whose byways we know, because we live there."[20] To be a bold and biblical people, we must renew our commitment to "living there." We must teach the Bible and reflect with our churches on how to use it in our personal and congregational lives. We need to have such teaching and reflection happen at all levels of our life together, from the preschoolers to the preachers.

There is widespread hunger for God's word, and in order to stay relevant, participants in the Reformed project must not be shy about what we have to offer. The Reformed principles of scriptural

interpretation are a gift from God given to meet the world's deep
need. As we use them may we be bold to claim our identity as a
biblical people who are living into God's vision for our own time
and place. May we clarify why it is not only right but necessary to
bring reason, experience, and tradition to bear on our reading of
the Bible—and then to go beyond merely learned interpretation of
Scripture to thinking interpretation. May we model a deep love and
respect for the Bible, even as we explain why we do not worship the
Bible or treat it as inerrant. And, finally, may we demonstrate generosity in our hearing of others' viewpoints and rejoice in the ties that
bind us even when the disagreements are sharp—knowing ourselves
to be united by the living Christ present in our midst, and heeding his
calls to repent of our old and sinful ways.

The Church Transforming

In the following essays, Michael Jinkins explores both the threats
and the opportunities facing the Reformed project at the present
time, in light of its rich history and tradition.

In chapter 1, "The Reformed Project," Jinkins explains why
he conceives of the work of the Reformed churches as a *project*
rather than simply a *set of traditions*. The word "tradition" refers
to things handed down, but the most important thing handed down
in the Reformed churches is not a body of propositional truths but
the actual work of reformation—"unfinished business," which must
be taken up by each new generation of believers. The core task of
the Reformed Project is to draw attention to Jesus of Nazareth, the
redeemer of creation in and through whom God is revealed, and to
ignite passion for living as his body in the world. This is what the
church has always taught.

In chapter 2, "What's Next for the Reformed Project?" Jinkins
contends that the church's relentless questions about what it can do
to guarantee its own survival are misguided, because Christ alone is
the church's savior. The questions we should be asking instead are,
Who is Christ? Who does Christ want us to be? and *How do we
articulate the gospel in this culture and in this time?* The gospel
teaches that we participate by faith in Jesus' own full and perfect

humanity and hence in God's original intention for us. But for us to be fully human we must also be in community, where we encounter and learn to embrace the differences that are essential to creation and reflected in God's own Trinitarian nature. And in Christian community we experience the reality of Christ's resurrection, which has the power to overwhelm us and make all things new.

In chapter 3, "Why a Thinking Faith Still Matters," Jinkins considers how John Calvin called a church that had descended into superstition and ignorance back to sound knowledge and wisdom. This foundational Reformed commitment to learning in service of faith has been demonstrated through the centuries by the founding of hospitals and universities around the world. Today the forces of superstition and ignorance are again rife, and there is urgent need for Christians to be able to deal with complex issues in suitably complex ways. The best response to the pervasive cultural barriers to thinking faith is for us to place the candle of scholarship on a lampstand instead of acquiescing by hiding it under a bushel. What is needed is a thinking faith in the service of faithful living—intelligence and faith linked together by a commitment to encourage the flourishing of human life and the promotion of justice.

Today we find our churches rent by a spirit of schism. In chapter 4, "Schism, the Unintended Consequence of the Reformed Project," Jinkins explores how the origins of this spirit lie in earliest Reformed church history. Schism, Jinkins argues, is a failure of love, a destructive habit of the heart based on an assumption that churches and individuals must separate from "unholy" and "unfaithful" coreligionists to maintain their own holiness and faithfulness. Though Calvin tried to hold the Church's unity in Christ in creative tension with the divisions that arose in the Reformers' struggles to be faithful, his invective against the Roman Catholic Church too often triumphed over acknowledgment of underlying unity. For Calvin's heirs it is the Reformed communion itself that becomes the object of anathemas. But the theological basis for unity also may be found in Calvin's writings, in his insistence that union with Jesus Christ is our only ground for union with one another.

In chapter 5, "Wonder, Spiritual Transformation, and Reformed Worship," Jinkins asks how our congregations can put the expectancy of a transforming experience of God at the heart of their life, worship, and mission. Since Christianity's inception, its claims to spiritual or mystical encounter have conflicted with more rational ways of approaching the divine. Church leaders today (both lay and ordained) must continue to manage this tension. To do so, they must recover the radical perspective of reverence in the presence of the sacred other even as they acknowledge that it is God alone who transforms and not they themselves who do so—their most creative efforts notwithstanding. The role of leaders is to serve as humble guides into the very mysteries of God—what Jinkins calls "docents in the house of wonder." As docents, leaders prepare people to encounter the divine, the Holy One of Israel, and help them to interpret their transformative experience.

In chapter 6, "Theological Education and the Reformed Project," Jinkins argues that we urgently need an educated clergy if we want to nurture a church that can grapple with the great challenges it faces. Theological education contributes to the church by conveying needed knowledge and teaching important ministerial skills, such as how to engage texts and traditions critically (the work of *informing*); by shaping people to become mature and wise leaders (the work of *forming*); and by pressing students to examine their deepest faith convictions critically yet faithfully, thus fostering change (the work of *transforming*). Magic happens in great theological education when a gifted teacher in love with her subject comes into contact with learners who are ready, "even when the readiness presents itself as a resistance to the subject" (p. 101). Such alchemy can occur in many seminary settings, but Jinkins celebrates especially those contexts where teachers and students are in community, living among one another and learning together.

In chapter 7, "A Forgotten Hallmark of the Reformed Project," Jinkins discusses how the Reformed project at its best has been marked by a kind of *innovation*—a capacity to adapt and change in new circumstances. Such innovation retrieves and reinterprets our rich legacy of Scripture and tradition; retains what is vital and necessary yet sheds what is nonessential or obsolete; exercises sacred imagination in order to see and convey with subtlety and power the wonder of the world and of God's ways; and ingeniously joins together people, things, and ideas that were unconnected, thus creating vibrant new ways to live our faith. To be sure, the Reformers saw themselves not as innovating but as restoring the church to its early simplicity and faithfulness of practice. Yet, their balance of fidelity and freedom with regard to tradition, their capacity for wonder, and their ingenious ability to make unexpected yet effective combinations are the very qualities that can carry us faithfully into the future.

In these essays, Michael Jinkins shows us that being a Reformed Christian today means, in many ways, what it has always meant. We trust in Jesus Christ, the one through whom God, by the power of the Spirit, makes us fully human. We trust in Christ, who shows us God's ways and brings us into God's very presence. We trust in Christ, who alone is the source of our unity. We trust in Christ, who makes us adventurous in the face of challenge and filled with hope and joy for what lies ahead.

Susan R. Garrett

Chapter 1

The Reformed Project

The Reformed faith is more an ongoing project than it is a tradition, a denomination, or even a communion, though it has elements of each of these. When we say, "We are Reformed," we are saying that we are Christians committed to a particular project. The Reformed project is concerned not so much with defining and defending such things as the uniqueness of a Reformed tradition as it is with recovering, in each new generation, Christian faith as God's calling of humanity to new life in Jesus Christ. Such a mission reflects the commitment of John Calvin "to renew the ancient form of the church." Whenever the Reformed movement has become preoccupied with itself it has missed the point of its existence. The Reformed project exists to draw our attention to Jesus of Nazareth in whom God is revealed and through whom God redeems creation.

A Call to Remember

We could chalk up the words Henry Chadwick spoke to the mutterings of a church historian who finds that his academic discipline has fallen out of favor. Or, maybe, his comment was inspired by the acrid taste of sour grapes. Perhaps he was simply another ecclesiastical leader watching his church go in a direction he would not have chosen. But there may have been more to it than that. Whatever the reason, his words found enough traction, enough staying power, that a journalist recalled what he said two decades later in his obituary. The journalist remembered the moment when in the midst of a debate in the Anglican Church's General Synod of 1988, Henry Chadwick, the eminent scholar and teacher, said, "Nothing is sadder than someone who has lost his memory, and the church which has lost its memory is in the same state of senility."[1]

Ironically, a couple of summers ago, while on a writing holiday in Scotland, I had just been mulling over Chadwick's words when I opened *The Daily Telegraph* and read an interview by Elizabeth Grice with Simon Schama, the historian. Schama, responding to the lack of historical instruction in Britain's secondary education, said, "A generation without history is a generation that not only loses a nation's memory, but loses a sense of what it's like to be inside a human skin."[2]

Every once in a while you come across an insight that galvanizes your own convictions. These two statements, from Chadwick and Schama, did that for me.

> "Nothing is sadder than someone who has lost his memory, and the church which has lost its memory is in the same state of senility," said Chadwick.

> "A generation without history is a generation that not only loses a nation's memory [and we could insert here 'a church's memory' or 'a peoples' memory'], but loses a sense of what it's like to be inside a human skin."

These two statements are profoundly connected, as anyone knows who has witnessed the debilitating malignancy of the mind we call Alzheimer's. When memory exits so goes our identity, our grasp on those particular and idiosyncratic recollections that make us who we are, that make us human, that hold us in relationship with one another, that not only make sense of our past but also orient us in the world. When memory fails us we are reduced to confusion. We cannot move forward because we have lost continuity with ourselves and with those who are closest to us. The question is why anyone — and more to the point I want to make — why any church would choose to jettison the memory that makes us who we are. Having loved and lost those who suffered from Alzheimer's, how could any of us wish for such a fate to befall our church?

I am sure that none of us would wish any such thing. And, yet, there are attitudes in our culture that seem to bless willful amnesia in the interest of being relevant—thereby undermining our ability to confront the challenges of the future with clarity. This is why our first step forward into what's next for the Reformed faith must be to *revitalize remembrance*.

Throughout this book, but especially in these first two chapters, I will invite us to remember a few specific things about the stream of Christianity to which many of us belong: the Reformed tradition, one of the four great Protestant traditions that sprang to life in the sixteenth century and continue to shape the faith of multitudes of Christians around the world.[3] This historical sketch will give us a better idea of where to go next.

We could remember many things about our history, but I will remind us first of that moment when John Calvin joined the Reformation of the Christian Church. To understand what is at stake in our own church and society, it is crucial for us to understand why Calvin and other Protestant reformers tried to reform the church.

A Church in Need of Reformation

The religious world into which John Calvin was born has so receded from our view that it is difficult now to imagine what it was like. Though western Europe was divided into kingdoms, the precursors of our modern nations, it was dominated by a single religious institution: the Roman Catholic Church. And while the Roman Catholic Church of the Middle Ages produced extraordinary and dynamic theologians (such as Duns Scotus and Thomas Aquinas) and was blessed by some of the most profound mystics and spiritual thinkers of all time (such as Julian of Norwich and Francis of Assisi), Europe was also a land where superstition and ignorance abounded, especially at the popular level. Ecclesiastical corruption, especially during the late medieval period, took advantage of both this superstition and this ignorance.

John Calvin, like many others before and after him, understood only too well that the church needed reformation to deliver it from the shackles of ignorance and superstition no less than it needed liberation from impiety and corruption. Some of Calvin's most vocal critics, in fact, agreed with him about the need to reform the church, though they were unwilling to endorse his Reformed solution to the problem.

Again, it's hard to get ourselves back into the worldview that dominated the medieval religious mind, but allow me for just a moment to give a glimpse of the superstition that masqueraded as religious faith, often attached to the big business of venerating and marketing relics (the mortal remains of the church's saints, believed by many to confer health and other blessings upon the faithful).

In the German city of Halle during the early sixteenth century, around the time the Protestant reformer Martin Luther came on the scene and a generation before our own John Calvin, pious Christians were told that venerating the bones of the saints in that city's cathedral would provide a reduction of no less than four thousand years in purgatory (an afterlife destination not mentioned in the Bible but taken for granted among the faithful of the Middle Ages).[4] This quantitative valuation, incidentally, was officially established by none other than Pope Leo X.

Alleged pieces of the cross, bits of the skull of John the Baptist and various bones of apostles, saints, and martyrs (together with innumerable counterfeit relics) were scattered across Europe. Clearly saints didn't rest much after death in the middle ages. They worked, and they worked hard, drawing pilgrims to sacred sites where prayers were supposed to be answered and wonders were said to be performed. When, for example, St. Cuthbert's body was dug up during the dismantling of monasteries under Henry VIII of England, they discovered, in addition to Cuthbert's bones, the head of an Anglo-Saxon king, skeletons of a number of infants, and another entire adult human skeleton all subletting Cuthbert's tomb. The idea was that being close to a dead saint conferred "spiritual" (i.e., quasi-magical) benefits.

Rome, of course, was the grand treasure trove and top trafficker of relics of saints. One historian provides the following portrait of Rome:

> Here in the single crypt . . . forty popes were buried and 76,000 martyrs. Rome had a piece of Moses' burning bush and three hundred particles of the Holy Innocents. Rome had a portrait of

Christ on the napkin of St. Veronica. Rome had the chains of St. Paul and the scissors with which Emperor Domitian clipped the hair of St. John. The walls of the Appian gate showed the white spots left by the stones which turned to snowballs when hurled by the mob against St. Peter. . . . A church in Rome had the crucifix which leaned over to talk to St. Brigitta. Another had a coin paid to Judas for betraying our Lord. . . . Still another church in Rome possessed the twelve-foot beam on which Judas hanged himself. . . . Above all, Rome had the entire bodies of St. Peter and St. Paul. They had been divided to distribute the benefits among the churches. The heads were in the Lateran, and one half of the body of each had been deposited in their respective churches.[5]

Superstition, under the cover of religious devotion, was rife in the medieval church. Carlos Eire, in his study *War against the Idols,* characterized late medieval religion as one that sought "to embody itself in images, reduce the infinite to the finite, blend the holy and the profane, and disintegrate all mystery."[6] Objects such as holy relics were seen as bearers of divine power for controlling nature and fending off mortality. A blurring of the lines between the spiritual, the sacramental, and the merely magical occurred, and, as Eire explains, "the clergy who controlled the *cultus* [the system of religious worship] offered little guidance on this point."[7]

Some Catholic scholars criticized the superstition of this popular religion. Some confronted the ignorance that supported such superstition. Others confronted those aspects of the ignorance of the people that were manifested in their lack of critical discernment: their deficits of knowledge and understanding both of biblical faith and of the world around them. Still others opposed the ecclesiastical corruption that took advantage of the popular ignorance and superstition. Many were convinced that the church desperately needed reforming. Warnings about the ignorance that fed superstition were not limited to scholars. Some ecclesiastical leaders in the Roman Catholic Church were also concerned about widespread ignorance among priests and laity—and had been for centuries. Almost three hundred years before the Protestant Reformation, for example, the documents agreed upon by the Provincial Synod of Lambeth (in 1281) critiqued "the ignorance of priests" that "precipitates the people into the pit of error."[8]

The portrait can be overdone (and has been by some Protestant propagandists), but there is more than a shade of truth in the caricature of an ignorant medieval priest muttering a sermon he did not write from a biblical text he could barely decipher, parroting the words of the Mass in a language he could not comprehend, in the presence of a people preoccupied by a magical deliverance from their considerable physical ills and the anxieties they bore under the threat of hell's furies and the drudgeries of purgatory.[9] There were many among the faithful for whom religion was more a matter of pious superstition than of spirituality and others for whom faith represented only the thinnest of veneers of outward devotion covering their baser interests.

There were some leading medieval Christians who raised the alarm and others who did their best to change the church's direction. Despite these warnings and efforts, however, it was not until the Renaissance and the work of humanists that an effective counter movement was mounted against the superstition, ignorance, and corruption that plagued the church and undermined authentic biblical faith. This is an important fact to recover in our self-understanding as Reformed Christians. There are some in our culture (both among Christians and among secularists) who use the word "humanism" to designate those who exclude even the possibility of God from human experience. But, there was a version of humanism that nourished the roots of the Reformation. In opposition to those who believed that the strength of Christianity lay in the ignorance (and hence the pliability) of its adherents (and, yes, really, this was the perspective of some church officials at the time), humanists like Erasmus wanted to translate the Bible from Greek and Hebrew into the vernacular languages of the people, so they could read and understand it for themselves. These humanists believed that the people's knowledge, not least their knowledge of the Bible, would dispel the fog of superstition, replacing magic with faith in God. Thus, in his introduction to the New Testament, Erasmus wrote,

> I utterly disagree with those who do not want the Holy Scriptures to be read by the uneducated in their own language, as though Christ's teaching was so obscure that it could hardly be understood even by a handful of theologians, or as though the strength of the Christian religion consisted in men's ignorance of it. I wish that

every . . . woman would read the Gospel and the Epistles of Paul. And I wish these were translated into each and every language, so that they might be read and understood not only by Scots and Irishmen, but also by Turks and Saracens. . . . I hope the farmer may sing snatches of Scripture at his plough, that the weaver may hum bits of Scripture to the tune of his shuttle, that the traveler may lighten the weariness of his journey with stories from Scripture.[10]

Along with Erasmus's passion for human knowledge we can hear in his words an evangelical fervor, a profound trust in the power of encountering the Bible as Word of God. We can hear, moreover, a confidence in the ministry of teaching, in education, in research and the acquisition of knowledge that would eventually become so important for our Reformed movement. A generation after Erasmus, for example, one unsympathetic visitor to a Reformed church in Lausanne, Switzerland, immediately noticed that "the interior arrangement of the edifice for worship" was "exactly like the interior of a school. Benches are everywhere and a pulpit for the preacher in the middle."[11] The Reformed project was, from its beginning, an educational project as much as an evangelical project, grounded in a confidence that knowledge of God and of God's word counteracted the religious anxiety which dominated the lives of people burdened by superstition and magic.[12] For the Reformers the school of Christ signaled a return to the sure knowledge and wisdom of the biblical text. Their radical reorientation and "spiritual return *ad fontes*, to the pure sources of scripture," as Eire observes, "required a more sophisticated clerical class to serve as interpreters, but also called for a more literate laity."[13] But, I'm getting ahead of myself.

Renaissance humanists believed that education should be biblical and theological in nature, but also more than that. In addition, knowledge of the great philosophers of ancient Greece and Rome should be offered, to help clear away the superstitious undergrowth that choked out the authentic piety of the church. They invited a larger public into a conversation that they already enjoyed with some of the greatest minds in history. Their humanism was inspired by a theological view of the world as God's creation. All wisdom, if it is true wisdom, comes ultimately from God, according to this version of humanism. All truth, whatever its source in the world, is authored by God. Jesus Christ is not only head of the church; Christ—the Word through whom all things are made—is also Lord of all creation. Thus, the knowledge of all humanity is vital to authentic faith. Epictetus (a Greek-speaking former slave who taught on the streets of ancient Hierapolis) and Seneca (an aristocratic Roman philosopher-statesman who wrote a series of elegant Latin letters and treatises) were potential sources of wisdom and truth for these humanists, alongside Athanasius (the great representative of fourth-century Christian orthodoxy whose brilliance shines through phrases of the Nicene Creed) and Bernard of Clairvaux (who combined spiritual devotion, intellectual prowess, and political savvy).

Perhaps it was in part a renewed engagement with the philosophical worldview that undergirded classical philosophy and its successors—a worldview that stressed tension between the material and the spiritual world—that provided some of the energy for humanism's critical stance toward superstition and ecclesiastical corruption. Perhaps even more it was the broad humanist education drawn from a variety of classical sources, some of which contradicted the Platonic separation of spirit and matter, that inspired the satire and parody that Erasmus and others employed to expose the corruption of medieval Christendom.[14]

Stories have long been told of hawkers of indulgences in the medieval Roman Church, stories especially about John Tetzel, arguably the most notorious peddler of indulgences in Germany. It was Tetzel's salesmanship that put the match to the fuse of Luther's Reformation. Tetzel worked in what we might today call the field of institutional development. He was raising funds for the expensive building projects of the Roman Church by selling the Pope's "plenary indulgences." By purchasing a "plenary indulgence," the Roman Church maintained, and Tetzel preached, Christians could receive a full and perfect remission of all their sins and "be restored to the state of innocence which they enjoyed in baptism," thus being "relieved of all the pains of purgatory." They could even secure these benefits for people already dead.[15] So arose the infamous marketing jingle linked to Tetzel's capital campaign:

> "As soon as the coin in the coffer rings,
> The soul from purgatory springs."[16]

It was in direct response to the practice of selling indulgences, specifically in reaction to Tetzel's entrepreneurship, that Martin Luther posted his Ninety-five Theses. Luther's challenge to the church's corruption was more narrowly focused than Erasmus's earlier indictment, but it was Erasmus who helped European intellectuals, the opinion shapers of the age, to see just how deep the church's corruption went and how dangerous its superstitions were.

Imagine a devoted Christian scholar equipped with the biting wit of Mel Brooks or Jon Stewart. Now mix this wit generously with the sharp argumentative genius of a first-rate trial lawyer. Then you have something like Desiderius Erasmus, a Renaissance scholar affiliated with the universities of Paris and Cambridge, a friend to the greatest and most devoted scholars of his age (like that "man for all seasons," Sir Thomas More). Erasmus's goal was "to use laughter to expose absurdity and corruption," and thus to provoke reform of the Roman Church from within the Roman Catholic Church.[17]

The most deliciously comic figure Erasmus portrayed was of a pope who was vainly trying to secure admittance to heaven. The scene was part of a play, *Julius Exclusus* (Julius Excluded), written anonymously (though everyone who was anyone knew the play was by Erasmus), published in 1517, just months before Martin Luther posted his Ninety-five Theses to the church doors in Wittenberg. While the scene is imaginary, the pope who gets ridiculed in Erasmus's book was real. He was Pope Julius II, often characterized as "the warrior pope," a disturbingly worldly figure.[18] One scholar notes, "The mounting clamor of anti-papal criticism, which was soon to swell into the Protestant Reformation, had long since taken this warlike pope as the very image of the diabolical Anti-Christ."[19]

The play centered on the comic-tragic scene of Pope Julius standing at the gates of heaven desperately trying to gain admittance, only to discover that his key wouldn't fit the lock. Julius's deeds, lampooned and ridiculed by Erasmus, were deadly serious. They epitomized a corrupt religious establishment dedicated to its own enrichment, pleasure, and survival while turning its back on Christ's mission.

Thoughtful scholars, statesmen, and church leaders throughout Europe agreed that the medieval Catholic Church needed reform, though they disagreed about how the reforms should be carried out. Erasmus, for example, feared that reform might turn into violent revolution and anarchy because of the forces unleashed by Martin Luther. Erasmus called Luther "the genius of discord."[20] That movement within the Roman Catholic Church commonly called the "Counter-Reformation," which represented a reaction against Protestantism, was itself a significant reformation of the Church. It was inspired by movements such as the Oratory of Divine Love (influenced by humanism), the Capuchins, and the Jesuits and culminated by the mid-sixteenth century in the Council of Trent (which addressed virtually every area of concern targeted by the Protestants, from ecclesiastical corruption to the lack of priestly education).

Luther himself, for all the changes he inspired, also feared the forces at work within the Protestant ranks. He could be particularly savage in his response to representatives of the Radical Reformation, the various Anabaptist groups. But Erasmus and Luther, as well as many others, understood that matters could not stand as they were in the church. The superstition that masqueraded as faith, the ignorance that made the superstition viable and prevented the people from reflecting critically on the faith they received, and the ecclesiastical corruption that fed off of both needed to be swept away.

This was something of the religious world into which John Calvin was born and in which he came to adulthood as a student of law and classical philosophy and literature. Twenty years after Luther's efforts gained steam and almost thirty years after Erasmus wrote his brilliant satires, Calvin stepped onto the world stage. Representing the second wave of the Protestant Reformation, he also represented, like Erasmus, the very best of Renaissance humanism. Calvin's first book, for example, was not a "religious" study, but a commentary on an essay by the Stoic philosopher Seneca. Like Luther, Calvin was also evangelical to the core. His greatest aspiration was to restore the church to its primitive faith and practice as taught in the Bible. As Calvin said in his letter to Cardinal Sadoleto, "All we attempted has been to renew the ancient form of the church."[21]

Calvin didn't plan to become a leader in the Reformation at all. He wanted only to be a private scholar. But he knew that the church needed reforming, and when William Farel detained him in Geneva with threats of God's fiery wrath should he deny God's call, Calvin allowed himself to abandon his own goal of private scholarship to take up the task of leading the church in Geneva. From there he inaugurated what we have variously described as "the Reformed movement" or "the Reformed tradition," but what I prefer to call "the Reformed project."

What Calvin sought to do was not to establish what we have come to call a denomination, but to perform a task. Calvin's project was to reform a church that had descended into superstition because ignorance had triumphed over sound knowledge and wisdom. He understood that an ignorant church in which superstition reigns is subject to corruption and vice. From the beginning his project was to reform this church.

A Deep and Personal Engagement with the Gospel

Because of the nature of the church's problems—ignorance and superstition—Calvin's tools for reforming the church were essentially educational. Calvin was and remained a teacher first and last. And he began to chop down the superstition that choked the church like kudzu, to slice away at the ignorance that nourished the superstition, and to call the church's leaders who benefited from the church's ignorance and superstition to account for their corruption. Founding and invigorating schools of all sorts, from church schools that taught the new Reformed catechisms to universities that encouraged new curricula and used the sharpest critical tools then available for scholarship (including critical methods to study the biblical text), Calvin and his colleagues sought to raise the educational level of the people, in the confidence that "sound and true wisdom and knowledge" would replace superstition with a deep, personal engagement with the gospel of Jesus Christ through the Bible. The project that Calvin began is our project to this day.

Thus, while I acknowledge that there is value in describing ourselves as members of "a Reformed communion" (especially when we think of the global connections among our churches) and in describing our deep aspirations and convictions as reflective of "the Reformed tradition" or "traditions," I would like to make a claim that initially may appear mystifying, but that (I hope) ultimately will prove clarifying: *The Reformed faith is more an ongoing project than it is a tradition, a denominational identity, or even a communion.*

When we say we are Reformed Christians, we are simply saying that we are Christians committed to a particular project, the project of reforming the church. As Calvin might say today, *all we are attempting is to continue to renew the authentic form of the church.*

Perhaps this sounds odd at first blush, but the Reformed project is concerned not so much with defining and defending such things as the uniqueness of a *Reformed tradition* or a distinctive *Reformed theology* over against other Christian "brands" as it is with *recovering the Christian faith as God's calling of humanity to new life in Jesus Christ.* Such a mission reflects precisely the commitment of John Calvin "to renew the ancient form of the church."

The Reformed project is less true to itself the more we think about our Reformed identity. And, conversely, the Reformed project is more truly Reformed the more it focuses on living and proclaiming the gospel of Jesus Christ.

Whenever the Reformed project has become preoccupied with itself it has missed the point of its existence. The Reformed project exists to draw our attention to Jesus of Nazareth in whom God is revealed and through whom God redeems and restores all creation. Our responsibility as Reformed Christians is to articulate Christian faith, what C. S. Lewis sometimes referred to as "mere Christianity."[22]

This does not mean that there are no distinctive features of what we might call "Reformed faith." There are particular emphases that have distinguished the Reformed approach to Christian faith from that of other Christians. But these Reformed emphases remain just that: *emphases.* The most distinctive aspect of the Reformed faith is also its most catholic, or universal: its unflagging commitment to articulate the gospel of Jesus Christ:

- That in Jesus of Nazareth, God's character is fully revealed; and in Christ, God reconciles Godself to the world;
- That in Jesus of Nazareth, sinners find forgiveness and are restored to that communion with God that is the essence of God's own life and love as Holy Trinity;

- That in Jesus of Nazareth, we are called to the ministry of reconciliation and justice, and the vocation of forgiveness that is God's mission in and to and for the whole world.

The Reformed Christian is more concerned with carrying on the project of recovering Christian faith from superstition and ignorance, fanatical excesses, popular reductionism, thoughtless distortions, and sick religion, than he or she is with trying to conform the church's theology with certain doctrines that John Calvin might have held five hundred years ago.

This point was made eloquently by Scottish theologian James Mackinnon who, in his study of Calvin, wrote: "[I]t is perhaps not superfluous to remind the perfervid Calvin Revivalists that our common Christian faith, as taught by its Founder [Jesus Christ], is not necessarily identical with any 'ism,' and that it is incumbent on His [Christ's] disciples to have recourse for themselves, in a free, if reverent, spirit to His teaching as its supreme and ultimate fountain and norm."[23]

This is the ongoing project that constitutes our lives as Reformed Christians. And it is this insistence on returning to our founder, Jesus Christ, that we need to recover from our past.

The Reformed project is exemplified in the portrayal of John the Baptist in Matthias Grünewald's famous painting of the crucifixion in the Isenheim altarpiece. We are called, like John the Baptist, to point away from ourselves toward Jesus Christ. For us, as for Calvin, in Jesus Christ all parts of our salvation are complete.

This is why the Reformed theologian Karl Barth kept a print of the crucifixion panel of the Isenheim altarpiece hanging above his desk. In the first volume of Barth's *Church Dogmatics*, Barth comments on that "prodigious index finger" of John the Baptist in this painting with which John points "away from himself" toward the crucified Christ.[24]

The entire Reformed project embodies John's gesture in this painting. The whole Reformed project functions like that "prodigious index finger," always pointing away from ourselves toward Jesus of Nazareth, reminding the world that Christian faith is not about us but about the love that God is and the grace that God reveals in Jesus of Nazareth.

As difficult as it is to remember, this is what the Reformed project demands that we never forget: Christian faith is not about our beliefs. And certainly it is not about our righteousness. Christian faith is not about our values. It is not about our interests. Christian faith is not even about our devotion, aspirations, hopes, and most pious dreams. *Christian faith is about the God revealed in Jesus Christ. Christian faith is about who this God is and what this God is doing in the world.* When we engage well in the Reformed project, we fulfill our vocation as witness-bearers to the good news of Jesus Christ. But when we become fixated on ourselves—though our motivations for doing so may be positive—we perform our project poorly.

Karl Barth is often remembered today as the greatest modern Reformed theologian. This is because Barth understood that in theological study, we are "always to begin anew at the beginning."[25] And, for Barth, as for all Reformed faith, the beginning point is not a concept or a principle but a name: Jesus Christ.[26]

To this end, Barth even protested against any attempt to found a theological school of thought or a movement that might advance his own way of thinking theologically, a fact that could bear remembering among some contemporary "Barthians." Barth writes,

> I would not like my life to result in the founding of a new school. I would like to tell anyone who is prepared to listen that I myself am not a "Barthian"; because after I have learnt something I want to remain free to go on learning. . . . Emphasize my name as little as possible. There is only one interesting name, and bringing up all the rest only leads to false loyalties, and can only arouse tedious jealousy and stubbornness among other people. . . . You will understand me correctly if you allow what I say to lead you to what he [Christ] says. A good theologian does not live in a house of ideas, principles and methods. He walks right through all such buildings and always comes out into the fresh air again.[27]

What Barth says here about his theological mission could be said with equal force for our entire Reformed project. The Reformed project exists only to bring us face-to-face with the gospel of Jesus Christ. It performs its task well to the extent that it prepares us to hear anew the Word of God. What we know as "distinctives" of the Reformed faith are simply beliefs we have affirmed with particular vigor, emphases we have placed on one or another Christian belief or commitment in the course of recovering Christian faith from superstition, ignorance, and abuse in every age since Calvin's.

When we say, for example, that one distinctive feature of the Reformed faith is the premium it places on education, on scholarship and disciplined thought, on the conviction that our love of God is somehow not entirely complete until we love God with our minds as well as with our hearts, souls, and strength, we are not saying that the Reformed faith is unique in valuing the intellect. Our frequently repeated quip that Presbyterians are "the Jesuits of Protestantism" only makes sense because there are also Jesuits of Catholicism. We are simply affirming that we Reformed Christians have found the quality of a "thinking faith" to be crucial in our continuing reformation of Christian faith. This distinctive is something we contribute to the life of the larger universal church.

John Calvin's Renaissance scholarship, for example, and the particular brand of skepticism that went along with Calvinist humanism was a tool in his hands to burn away the clutter of superstition from the worship of Christians in his own time. Calvin understood how the actions of an ignorant and poorly educated clergy played a key role in the corruption of the medieval church. Calvin countered superstition, ignorance, magic, and corruption with deep, careful, critical theological thought, insisting that those who preached the Word of God should be disciplined in their critical study of the Bible and that their understanding of faith should be tempered with a deep acquaintance with centuries' worth of careful theological reflection. Thus when we witness in our own time the ways in which an ignorant Protestantism proves its piety by assuming that it speaks unequivocally for God, we are reminded that it is only a single generation of poor theological and biblical training that separates us all from fundamentalism and fanaticism. The fact that scholarship has remained a defining feature of the Reformed project is related directly to the value of knowledge in dispelling the smoke and mirrors of bad religion and for creating a hearing for the gospel.

One further example: We often think of resistance to idolatry as a Reformed theological distinctive. And it is true that opposition to idolatry has been emphasized by the Reformed faith. But the fact that the Reformed project has historically attacked idolatry in its various forms is directly related to the Reformed faith's commitment to recovering the Christian understanding that the worship of idols inevitably enslaves us to the powers and principalities of the world marketing themselves falsely as "God."

Calvin was iconoclastic (literally, an "image breaker," or an "idol breaker") in the narrow and technical sense, because he rooted out idolatry, whether in the form of the worship of figurines made by human hands or the veneration of relics. But Calvin was also iconoclastic in the broader and more metaphorical sense, calling Christians away from the worship of any *thing* in place of God.

Centuries after Calvin, when Karl Barth and his Lutheran and Evangelical colleagues in Germany published their Theological Declaration of Barmen in opposition to Nazism, they were not simply affirming a set of Reformed or even Protestant principles. They were reclaiming basic universal, or catholic, Christian beliefs regarding the character and authority of the God revealed in Jesus Christ, and they were doing so in direct contradiction to the Nazi party's totalitarian and therefore idolatrous attempts to assume authority over all aspects of human existence. In the name of the liberating power of the gospel, the framers of the Barmen Declaration were protesting the power of idolatry to enthrall humanity.

When Barth and his compatriots confessed "Jesus Christ, as he is attested for us in Holy Scripture, is the one Word of God which we must hear and which we have to trust and obey in life and in death,"[28] they were not subscribing to a peculiar Reformed tenet but to the common belief of Christian faith. On behalf of Christianity and for the sake of Christianity (and, indeed, for the sake of human society), their Reformed project was to recover a belief that was, at that moment, under considerable threat by the idolatrous powers supported by the false mythologies of nationalism, racism, and blood.

If we were to visit every distinctive of the Reformed faith, we would find not something unique to Presbyterians or other Reformed Christians, but a conviction held in common with all Christianity: a belief, a perspective on the Christian adventure that we as Reformed Christians have emphasized (sometimes with particular or peculiar force), but always for the sake of the whole gospel of Jesus Christ and the whole church and the whole of creation. This is the essential theological feature of the Reformed project. For example,

- To speak of the sovereignty of God (which is held by many to be the most distinctively Reformed theological "distinctive") means, in part, to announce the reign of God promised in the Old Testament and incarnate in Jesus of Nazareth. It also affirms the universal Christian teaching that God is ultimately "in charge," "sovereign," over all.

- To speak of original sin or total depravity is to recognize the persistence of those forces in human nature that have undercut our best efforts, our highest motives, and our grandest aspirations, those tenacious and malignant aspects of our own lives that never do escape the vortex of self-centeredness, pride, and self-interested failure to love, as well as the social and structural aspects of the "powers and principalities" of our world that fail to ensure justice, peace, and mercy. We find this doctrine lived out from the story of Adam and Eve to the front page of yesterday's newspapers. While Presbyterians have often reminded Christianity of sin's tenacity, we don't own a copyright on original sin.

- To confess the irresistibility of God's grace is to reaffirm the Christian belief that no power under heaven is greater than God's power to redeem; that even the forces of sin, suffering, evil, and death yield ultimately to God's grace. This we hold in common, in some form or the other, with Christians from the fourth century's Gregory of Nyssa to contemporaries like Douglas John Hall and Serene Jones. While Reformed Christians have articulated this doctrine distinctively, Christians since the apostle Paul have affirmed that nothing "will be able to separate us from the love of God in Christ Jesus our Lord" (Rom. 8:38–39).

- To affirm the Lordship of Jesus Christ, the reconciling work of God in Christ, our election to eternal life in Christ, God's providential care, the call to do justice, love mercy, and walk humbly with God, the authority of holy Scripture, the means of grace made available to us in the Bible, prayer, and sacraments is to articulate touchstones belonging to all Christianity and not the unique features of one particular Christian sect, though, again, the Reformed project has articulated each and all of these doctrines with its own distinctive accent.

To be Reformed is just to be a Christian who has taken on a particular project, a task, a mission for the sake of Christianity and in continuity with certain historical streams.

Theologically, this Reformed project rests in God's completed work in Christ. *Pragmatically*, it can never rest from its commitment to recover and articulate again and again, in and for each new generation, the gospel of Jesus Christ.

Chapter 2

What's Next for the Reformed Project?

The purpose of the Christian faith, from a Reformed perspective, is not to make us religious. God did not go to all the trouble of becoming a human being just to teach us an official club handshake. The Reformed project seeks to recover the core Christian conviction that God became human to make us human—like Jesus of Nazareth. The Reformed project has dedicated itself to recovering this understanding because it is a—perhaps *the*—fundamental teaching of Christian Scripture. "What's next for the Reformed project" is much more than merely a recovery of certain theological affirmations: it is a recovery of the life of faith in Christian community as an expression of the life of the triune God, and a retelling of the message of the resurrection as God's imprimatur upon the life of trust and obedience lived by Jesus—a life that culminates in the cross.

The Quest for the Right Question

In the previous chapter we remembered the beginnings of the Reformed project, particularly the ways in which John Calvin sought to burn away the underbrush of superstition, the ignorance that nourished it, and the corruption that fed on it. Calvin's goal was to restore the church to its primitive simplicity, the authenticity and faith of the church of Jesus' earliest followers. In this chapter I draw further on Calvin and other reformers to recover the core theological concern of Christian faith: *living the life for which God created us.*

19

To understand why we need to address something as basic as this, I want to share a joke that is not funny and a reflection from someone who is not officially part of the Reformed movement.

First, the joke that is not funny. Question: What do you get when you cross a Presbyterian with a Jehovah's Witness? Answer: Someone who reluctantly goes door to door and has no idea what to say when a door opens.

Second, the reflection from someone who isn't Reformed but from whom we have a lot to learn: Dietrich Bonhoeffer. Recently I began reading a new translation of Bonhoeffer's "Lectures on Christology." You can find it in volume 12 of Bonhoeffer's Works.[1] I recommend these lectures for many reasons, but the most important reason is because Bonhoeffer actually believed that something is at stake when we make theological statements: that is, when we try to make statements about God. Bonhoeffer believed that something crucial hangs in the balance when we preach and speak about God, and so we should be careful with our words.

Whereas we often rush to speak in this culture, acting like zealous school children thrusting our hands into the air and waving them about to get the attention of the teacher, eager to show off that we have the answer, Bonhoeffer struggles—again and again—to get the question exactly right. He objects to the "prattle" of the merely religious. "The silence of the church is silence before the Word. In proclaiming Christ," he says, "the church falls on its knees in silence before the inexpressible. . . . To speak of Christ is to be silent, and to be silent about Christ is to speak."[2]

Bonhoeffer waits and listens in the presence of God's Word to learn what to say about the Word who is God. Out of this deep silence a profound understanding emerges. Bonhoeffer believes that there is such a thing as the right question. The right question, he says, is "the question asked by horrified, dethroned human reason." It is "also the question of faith." And it is the question we must ask the Word, Jesus Christ. Bonhoeffer asks Jesus Christ, the incarnate Word of God: "Who are you? Are you God's very self?"

Bonhoeffer protests against our tendency to let the decisive theological question, "Who are you?" dissolve into questions about "how": How is this possible? How can God be like this? How can Christ be human and divine? The how questions are the fragmenting, mechanical, manipulating questions, the debilitating questions about mere techniques and technologies, How? How? How?

Bonhoeffer, by contrast, tenaciously sticks to the "Who" question, as he calls it. He explains that "the place where our work must begin is clearly indicated. In the church, where Christ has revealed himself as the Word of God," we ask the question: *Who are you, Jesus Christ?* "The answer is given. The church receives it every day anew." It is up to us, Bonhoeffer continues, "to understand the question as it is given, and to reflect upon and analyze it as it exists. But it remains always the question, 'Who.'"[3]

You can't come up with the right answers until you get the right question. The great question facing our church is not, *What can the Reformed tradition do to ensure that it has a future?* Or, even worse, *How can we guarantee the survival of the Presbyterian Church?* Rather, the right questions are, *Who is Christ?* and *Who does Christ want us to be?*

These are the questions that drive, inform, and shape all our other questions. These are the questions the Reformed project must ask for one simple reason: *we know the church is not ours.* The church does not belong to us. The church belongs to Jesus Christ, the Lord of creation and head of the church. And, despite the compulsions that emerge in our latter day Pelagianism (i.e., our perverse and tragic conviction that we shall be saved *by our own works* and we shall save the church *by our own works*), the church does not need us to save it. The church has a savior already. And at least one reason we languish in anxiety today is because our focus has shifted ever so subtly, but ever so crucially, from Christ to us. The more anxious church leaders have become in recent years—whether their anxiety is driven by changes in demographics or popular culture or moral codes—the more our attention has tended to shift from Christ to us. Ernst Käsemann articulated this perspective well when he argued, "Wherever ecclesiology moves into the foreground, however justifiable the reasons may be, Christology will lose its decisive importance, even if it does so by becoming integrated, in some form or other, in the doctrine of the church, instead of remaining the church's indispensable touchstone."[4]

Therefore, when we think about what is next for the Reformed project, we must think first about what it means for this project to recover and articulate the gospel of Jesus Christ in this culture and in this time—the gospel that will form the content of our proclamation and shape our liturgy, the work of the people of God (both in worship and in obedient service in the world). To find an answer, we must go to the heart of the human dimensions of the "Who" question. We must recast the Reformed project as a recovery of a Christian understanding of human life. I am saying that what is next for the Reformed project is first and foremost a theological task. And because it is a theological task, it is also and at the same time, a homiletical task, a liturgical task, and an educational task. But, ironically, in every case, it is the task of pointing persistently away from ourselves and our preoccupations to Jesus Christ as God's self-revelation.

Reforming an Understanding of the Christian Life as (Simply) a Truly Human Life

I begin with what may be the most comprehensive and yet humble theological claim made by John Calvin and others reforming Christian faith, that *the Christian life is simply human life lived fully as God intended.* Christian life is human life flourishing in utter dependence on God—human life empowered by God's Spirit.

Calvin's claim does not mean that Christians "have got it right" and all others have it wrong. It means, instead, that the call of Jesus of Nazareth to live abundantly, to trust God, to hold our lives and our survival lightly, and to follow Jesus restores us to the humanity for which God created us in the first place. The Reformed project has historically insisted that we place our emphasis on trustful living rather than on religion. The purpose of the Christian faith, from a Reformed perspective, is not to make us more religious but to make us human, like Jesus.

To put it even more bluntly, the Reformed project seeks to recover the Christian idea that God did not go to all the trouble of becoming a human being just to teach us an official club handshake. We are recovering the bold theological claim that the full humanity restored in Jesus Christ by the power of the Holy Spirit is the same humanity God shares with us through Christ in the power of the Spirit. This imparting to us of authentic human nature is a matter of far more consequence than religion. It was for this purpose that God became flesh, not to establish a new religion.

Religion can be good, bad, or indifferent. Religion can be healthy or sick. Religion can be beautiful and life-giving or violent and deadly. Religion can even be true or false. Religion can be a powerful expression of the human need to acknowledge the presence of God and to order our lives in a manner consistent with the God who created us. But religion can also be a woeful expression of a compulsive desire to manipulate our environment and other persons to get what we want.

Whatever religion is, it is not God's endgame in this world, at least not according to Christian faith.[5] God became human to make us human. The Reformed project has dedicated itself to recovering this understanding because it is a fundamental teaching of Christian Scripture—perhaps *the* fundamental teaching of Christian Scripture. From this teaching flows our perspective on creation (as that which God loves and restores in love and calls us to tend as stewards), ethics (as the realm of goodness and grace, forgiveness and justice in relationships among all persons and institutions), worship (as the essential act of rendering to God that which honors and glorifies God), and evangelism (as a simple sharing with others of the good news of God's love and generosity).

The Reformed project also, however, takes issue with certain expressions of the religious impulse popularly called "spirituality"—at least those forms of "spirituality" that are characterized by an inward-looking preoccupation of the self with the self in the name of God. While there are varieties of "spirituality" that are richly conceived responses to the mystery and holiness of God, generous and open to others, and profoundly oriented to the life of the Spirit of God in all its fullness, there are also shallow and self-absorbed varieties. These amount to little more than attempts to find a feeling of transcendence without recognizing the objective "wholly otherness" of the transcendent God who calls us to "do justice and love mercy" as well as to walk with God. The Reformed project has often raised concerns about such forms of religion or "spirituality."[6]

One of John Calvin's biggest arguments (at least in print) was with Andreas Osiander, a Lutheran theologian, who could be a poster child for some of the least edifying varieties of today's popular "spirituality." "Osiander's life," according to John T. McNeill, "was a succession of controversies."[7] And his controversy with Calvin was a knock-down-drag-out right across the pages of Calvin's classic introduction to Christian faith, his *Institutes*.

Basically, Osiander taught that the goal of the Christian faith is for us to receive the essence of God's nature. He believed that through our faith in Jesus Christ we are infused with deity—that God actually shares with us the divine nature of Christ. His idea finds a parallel in spiritual writers today (whether Christian or pagan) who affirm "the divine" in each of us.

Calvin would have none of this. According to Calvin, Osiander is missing the point of what God is doing in the incarnation of Jesus Christ. God is not trying to make little deities of us. God is making us human. God is restoring us to the humanity that God intended for us at the time of creation. We do not receive some ephemeral spiritual or abstract divine essence from Jesus Christ. Rather, we participate by faith in the *humanity* of Jesus Christ so that we can be restored through the power of the Holy Spirit to God's original intention for humanity, remembering that the Spirit at work in us is the same Spirit who was at work in Jesus of Nazareth.[8]

The love, trust, faith, authenticity and truth, joy and vulnerability, freedom and obedience to God's reign that we see in Jesus of Nazareth constitute the life God intends for us all. Jesus did not "snatch at equality with God."[9] Jesus embraced his humanity, entrusting himself fully to God in life and in death. Not even the most acceptable moral laws of his religion came between Jesus and his radical obedience to God, as we learn from the many stories of his conflicts over the Sabbath or over laws related to ritual cleanliness and diet.[10]

The Reformed project sees the wisdom and the sanity of embracing our nature as creatures and of never forgetting the "infinite qualitative difference" between God and us.[11] We are called to live with reverence in the presence of God and to rest in God's sovereign reign over creation, entrusting ourselves and all we love to God's parental care and participating by the power of God's Spirit in what God is doing in the world.

This is why the Reformed project has placed so much emphasis on the *humanity* of Jesus Christ, even while it also affirms his full divinity. For Calvin, "Christ is the mirror of our sanctification."[12]

If we want to know who and what we truly are, if we want to know our real identity and God's ultimate purpose for our lives, we don't look in the bathroom mirror; we look into the human face of Jesus of Nazareth. When we look into the face of Jesus, we see the human being who lived precisely the life God intended for all humanity, for *our* humanity, a life lived in utter dependence on God, trusting in God, obedient to God in each moment—we see a human being who was crucified because he lived this sort of life in this sort of world. And it was upon this particular human life, fully lived even unto death on a cross, that God placed God's unqualified seal of approval in the resurrection.

So it was that Lesslie Newbigin observed that the cross is not the emblem of a defeat reversed on Easter morning. Easter is the confirmation of a victory won in a life culminating in the cross, a life lived as God intended.[13] It is for this quality of human life that God created us. It is to this quality of human life that God calls us. It is for the living of this quality of human life that God shares with us God's Spirit, the Spirit of Christ.

This, according to the Reformed project, is the good news—the gospel that we are called to live and to speak. As George MacLeod, founder of the Iona Community, once said, "We are to be to others what Christ has become for us."[14] And if we want to understand what Christ has become for us, we have only to look at the cross, not as a religious symbol, but as a symbol of a life lived trusting God for the outcome.

In his remarkable book *Only One Way Left*, MacLeod continued by saying,

> I simply argue that the Cross be raised again at the centre of the market-place as well as on the steeple of the church. I am recovering the claim that Jesus was not crucified in a cathedral between two candles, but on a cross between two thieves; on the town garbage-heap; at a crossroad so cosmopolitan that they had to write his title in Hebrew and in Latin and in Greek . . . ; at the kind of place where cynics talk smut, and thieves curse, and soldiers gamble. Because that is where He died. And that is what He died about. And that is where [we] should be and what [we] should be about.[15]

This is the voice of the Reformed project for our time, a full-throated recovery of the message of the liberating power of the gospel.

As a young woman in Nashville recently said to me, the time has come for the church to realize that church membership is not about attending a meeting at a particular time each week. It is about more, much more. It is about living a particular quality of life, a human life. Among the things that are "next" for the Reformed project, there is a recovery of the Christian understanding of a Christian life as a fully human life, an understanding that liberates the church to see its mission anew.

A Reformed Recovery of Community

Religion can become obtusely institutionalized, even to the point that the concerns and needs of persons play second fiddle to the interests of ecclesiastical structures and the tangled rights and privileges of offices. And spirituality can become isolated, privatized, and self-obsessed, sometimes reinforcing the powers and principalities that oppress humanity in exchange for leaving the individual's so-called spiritual interests alone. But, in contrast to these, the Reformed project recovers the Christian understanding that we can only be fully human in community. We can't be human alone.

John Calvin understood the life of faith as a life lived in community. Karl Barth, in a logical extension of Calvin's thought, understood even the most basic relationships of life (such as the love between two persons) as a reflection of God's own being-in-relationship as Father, Son, and Holy Spirit. It took other representatives of the Reformed project, however, from Emil Brunner to Kathryn Tanner to take this perspective a step further, helping us see how our understanding of the church is a creaturely reflection of the triune God.[16]

The Reformed project recovers the Christian understanding that we cannot be human as God intended without being human together. We need one another in order to be human, because humanity is created in the image of God, and the God in whose image we are created is not the distant, isolated, quasi-divine principle espoused by some seventeenth-century rationalists or the cold, detached metaphysical watchmaker of eighteenth-century Deism, but the loving, vulnerable, suffering God revealed in Jesus Christ. We need one another in order to be human, because human beings are formed and shaped in and through communities. We are formed and we are transformed through the crucible of mutual admonition, through forgiveness and forbearance, through a process that (to use an old and biblical word) "edifies" us, or "builds us up" into persons of faith.

What's next for the Reformed project is as countercultural as you can get in this increasingly atomistic and isolated age. Flesh and blood need contact with flesh and blood in order to flourish. Humanity cries out for humanity. We cannot grow up into the full stature of Christ if alone. Nor can we thrive without the differences of one another.

Our differences provide the friction that sculpts us into human shape. We need to know and be known. There has never been a time when the mournful words of Captain Ahab in Melville's *Moby-Dick* were more poignant or more true: "Close! stand close to me, Starbuck; let me look into a human eye; it is better than to gaze into sea or sky; better than to gaze upon God."

Rather than treat the differences among us as a plague, we can treat them as an inestimable gift. But to do this we must cultivate a spirit of generosity toward our differences. And this spirit of generosity only makes sense if we believe that God is the author of our differences, that the variety woven into creation is the consequence of a God who loves freedom more than security.

Creation could never be as rich and full as it is without the proliferation of difference. Nor can we become all we are meant to be without the differences among us. Our differences are not simply the result of an accident; they are essential to God's creation. The diversity of the world around us reflects God's own eternal being (Father, Son, and Holy Spirit)—God's diversity in union, God's apparent delight in variety. If God were the singular, isolated, distant monad some philosophers take God to be, then it would make sense that all reality, all of creation, and our humanity would be just as singular, just as isolated and distant from others, just as bare. But God is not that at all, not if God really is revealed in Jesus of Nazareth through the power of the Holy Spirit. God's own being is holy Trinity, the tri-unity of Father, Son, and Holy Spirit—Lover, Beloved, Love. God's very being is in relationship, eternally: the Father is the eternal source of all being; the Son is the eternal, self-giving, imageless image of the Father; the Spirit is the eternal life and love whom God the Father and God the Son share with one another, and from whom God creates all that is. The triune God, whose being consists in the mystery of diversity in unity, created the world, including humanity, from the depths of God's own love and life, from the depths of God's startling generosity and overflowing delight in variety, and placed upon all creation the indelible stamp of God's own triune character. Diversity among us—along with the differences that are inseparable from diversity—is not something we simply tolerate. It is something we enjoy, delight in, glory in, and bless.

Learning to bless and not curse difference is one of the first steps to learning to bless God's creation. Learning to bless and not curse variety is one of the first steps in learning to understand and accept what it means for us to be created in the image and likeness of God. Learning to bless and not curse diversity is one of the first steps in learning to cultivate community that nurtures our full humanity in Christ.

The Church's Ministry as Theology's Polygraph

Alan Lewis, a theologian who was more dedicated to the Reformed project than almost anyone I have ever known, once observed, "Ministry is theology's polygraph, its infallible lie-detecting test, revealing the truth of what the church believes and the identity of whom she worships—the God of the cross or the false deities of her cultural ideology."[17]

What did Alan mean when he wrote these words? In what sense is the church's ministry theology's polygraph?

Do our busy programs and our worrisome zeal, our pursuit of pop entertainment in the guise of the worship of God, our "user-friendly," yet biblically uninformed, spiritually vapid sermons, and market-driven responses to religious consumerism genuinely have a story to tell to the nations, or do they only testify to the vacuity of our theology? We cannot simply disconnect the church's ministry (what we pragmatically do to serve the institutional needs of the church) from our essential beliefs, from the hopes and aspirations, from the fundamental understandings of who God is and whom we are called to be in Jesus Christ, can we?

Perhaps, the problem is with our hopes and aspirations themselves. Have we become conditioned to hopes too small? Have our
aspirations grown stunted by our fears and anxieties? Strapped to a
lie detector of our own theological making, ought our contemporary
church to sweat?

We are haunted by the specter of the church's indentured servi-
tude to the culture's standards of success, by the enduring temptation to trim the church's ministry and mission so as to cause neither
scandal to the world's sensibilities nor shock to its values. But we are
also aware, in our best moments, that culture and world, along with
all principalities and powers, also belong to God, are also part of
God's good creation, and though they are fallen (as is all of creation,
including the institutional church), they possess enormous redemptive potential in Christ.

The crisis in which we find ourselves is fueled by our anxieties. We
appear to believe that we can save the church's institutional life by
appropriating some of our culture's least savory aspects, by abandon-
ing the message of the cross of Jesus Christ for a superficial message
of self-improvement, or by rejecting the good news of the resurrection
in Christ for a gospel of financial wealth. As one consultant said to
a group of theologians (of which I was one), "If you want people to
come to church, you've got to put on a good show. Like Jesus did!
You've got to do some tricks. Turn water into wine. That will put butts
back on the pews!" A church preoccupied with mere survival might
be willing to do anything, might sacrifice anything, even the cross of
Jesus, to stave off institutional death. It might be willing to agree to
any temptation (bread, power, fame; see Matt. 4:1–11).

Perhaps there has never been a better time in the church's history
for the Reformed project to recover Christ's words that have pursued
us down through time like the hound of heaven:

> Then he began to teach them that the Son of Man must undergo
> great suffering, and be rejected by the elders, the chief priests, and
> the scribes, and be killed, and after three days rise again. . . . "If
> any want to become my followers, let them deny themselves and
> take up their cross and follow me. For those who want to save their
> life will lose it, and those who lose their life for my sake, and for
> the sake of the gospel, will save it. For what will it profit them to
> gain the whole world and forfeit their life?" (Mark 8:31–36).

A church preoccupied with survival might do anything to avoid its crosses. But, the church of Jesus Christ does not merely survive. The church lives in the power of the resurrection. The church suffers and the church dies following our Lord. The church bears its crosses for the sake of Christ and his gospel over and over again in history. And God raises the church from every death. That is our hope.

This is what it means, after all, to say, with the Second Helvetic Confession, that the church "will always exist." It is not a statement of mere optimism or of confidence in the church's resources, because the church that *we* can save, the church that just survives, would not be the church of the crucified Christ. To say that the church "will always exist" is to confess (and to confess radically) our trust in God's faithfulness to raise the church from every death.

Witnesses at the Door

There have been, in recent years, a number of unhelpful exercises in which the church and its leaders have participated. I have sat in more rooms than I care to remember when the anxiety and fear rippled through the audience like waves across a lake, as respected leaders (and some popular consultants) have tried to convince their hearers of the rightness of their diagnoses, the correctness of their solutions, or the magical power of their snake oil. One of the more useful exercises in which we have participated, however, has been the attempt by some other respected leaders to discern the right biblical analogy to help us illuminate our contemporary situation as a church.

A few years ago as mainline Protestants first began to settle into the new reality of our numerical decline—the so-called dis-establishment era for Protestantism in North America—some leaders described us as living in an age of exile. I recall Jack Stotts, then president of Austin Presbyterian Seminary, reflecting eloquently on this theme. The judgment and grace of exile, the astonishing fruitfulness of faith that occurred during the exile, the transformative power of exile—all were explored, enabling us to see our current situation through new eyes.

Recently my colleague and friend, Cynthia Campbell, past president of McCormick Theological Seminary in Chicago, used Exodus

14:10–15 to shine light on our present situation. She sees our current state through the lens of that moment when Moses and the people stood with their backs against the sea and their faces turned to the Egyptian armies of Pharaoh. The people complained to Moses: "Was it because there were no graves in Egypt that you have taken us away to die in the wilderness? . . . It would have been better for us to serve the Egyptians than to die in the wilderness" (Exod. 14:11–12).

This passage from Exodus, as you may remember, ends with the Lord God saying to Moses, "Why do you cry out to me? Tell the Israelites to go forward" (v. 15). I think Cynthia is right. This passage has a lot to say to us today.

For some time, however, another analogy has been rattling round my brain, and I offer it because I think our situation is complex enough that it needs a variety of biblical analogies to illuminate it well. I have been reflecting on that moment in the life of the fledgling Christian movement when we believed every hope lay dead and buried in the tomb of Joseph of Arimathea. (We get glimpses of this moment in Luke 24:1–12 and John 20.)

The disciples are huddled in a room in Jerusalem, hunkered down, worried about their respective futures, anxious about the future of the messianic movement to which they have been attached as followers of Jesus of Nazareth. Their charismatic young teacher was crucified by the Romans. He has been in the cold grave for three days. We can only imagine the topics of conversation in that room, the tension and the fear thick among them. "Is this movement to suffer the fate of John the Baptist's followers after his death? Will we just scatter?" they worried. "Are the Romans planning, even now, to come after us? Will we share the fate of Jesus?" they wondered. "Remember when hundreds gathered to listen to Jesus? Remember when so many came that we couldn't find food for them all? Remember the children shouting 'hosanna' as he rode into Jerusalem, and we thought the kingdom of God on earth was right around the corner? Remember when we built that huge educational addition because so many wanted to attend Sunday school?" (Oops, strike that last one!)

So much they had hoped for was clearly over. Their aspirations had evaporated.

Peter, perhaps, contemplated buying a new fishing boat. Levi wondered if maybe he could get his old job as a tax collector back.

Simon the Zealot eyed his political prospects in light of the changing forecast. John and James tried to figure out what they were going to tell their mother about their professional options now that sitting on the right and left hand of the Messiah had lost its luster.

What a contrast to the mood in the room where they met the night before Jesus' execution, when they dined with Jesus, and prayed with Jesus, and pledged themselves to walk with Jesus. Now he was dead and their hopes with him.

The irony is that, at some point, even while they were huddled anxiously in that room, the resurrection had already happened. Jesus had already risen from the dead. Even as their aspirations were unable to grasp the message of his death, their hopes could not stretch large enough to conceive of the impossible possibility of his resurrection.

It is so easy to blame those first disciples for not having a hope big enough to encompass resurrection. But that is really a cheap shot. They merely knew what they knew. Dead is dead. Gone is gone. Impossible is impossible. "Let's get real," you can almost hear one of them say, "whatever dreams we had are buried in Joseph's tomb. We just have to face facts."

Whenever I hear someone say that the situation we face in the church today is graver and more challenging than any we have ever faced before, I have to stifle a laugh. Our low point surely was at the very beginning of the Christian movement. As the disciples of Jesus muttered and worried in that room long ago, they could not imagine that Christ was raised from the dead, risen with healing in his wings. Nor could they imagine that his death and resurrection had judged even their highest aspirations as inadequate and had pronounced their greatest hopes as infinitely too small, as faithless.

There was a knock at the door of that room in which the disciples huddled. Women knocked at the door, fresh from the tomb with incredible news.

Do we hear the knock at the door today?

There are witnesses fresh from the empty tomb. They have run here. They are out of breath. They have news for us, good news for us. Christ is raised from the dead. This is news too big for our hopes, news that calls into question all our prior hopes. This is news that makes our doubts and anxieties obsolete. This is news that requires new plans. It always has.

Rather than returning to their fishing boats and tax offices, their swords and visions of glory, the disciples long ago spread out across their world with this good news on their lips, building new communities of persons whose worlds were turned upside down by this impossible gospel, new communities baptized into the death of Christ and raised into a new life with its own new identity that trumped every old difference that divided them in the world.

Do we hear the knock of witnesses at the door?

"What's next for the church?" we ask again and again. "What's next for the Reformed project?"

This is what's next: Resurrection.

Resurrection is next. Resurrection is next, and it has already happened. Resurrection is next, and it has the power to overcome and overwhelm everything around us, to make all things new, to make us think new thoughts and imagine new possibilities and make new plans.

Do we hear the knock of witnesses at the door?

Do we have the courage to open the door?

Chapter 3

Why a Thinking Faith Still Matters

One of the greatest gifts of the Reformed project is its commitment to the life of the mind in the service of God. From the first, Reformed Christians have sought to advance the best thinking in the face of superficiality, superstition, bad religion, social reactivity, and anxiety. As expressions of confidence that Christian faith and the promotion of knowledge go hand-in-hand, the Reformed project established the first programs of universal education, founding universities, graduate schools, and teaching hospitals as it moved across the world. Today the world's problems have become extraordinarily complex, and many religious people try to prove their religious devotion by refusing to test their convictions intellectually or by seeking to silence those with whom they disagree. Now more than ever, we as Reformed Christians must foster the curiosity and intellectual openness that have driven us to think deeply, for there is desperate need for faithful people who are bold and unflinching thinkers, people who will use their best knowledge and concerted intellect to engage and mend a broken world.

A Besieged Value

A generation ago the arguments advanced in this chapter about the importance of a thinking faith would have seemed so obvious they would have required no rehearsal at all, let alone any defense. But something has changed.

Nicholas Kristof, a columnist for *The New York Times*, wrote an essay a few years ago in which he mourned the passing of an intellectually rigorous faith. The American public at large, according to Kristof, has grown increasingly credulous. By contrast, he remembers his grandfather, "a devout and active Presbyterian elder," who regarded the virgin birth as a more or less legendary aspect of the Christian faith and evolutionary theory as a sensible scientific explanation of how nature works. Kristof writes, "Those kinds of mainline Christians are vanishing," and they are being replaced by Christians who are either unable or who simply refuse to prove the fervor of their religious convictions by testing those convictions intellectually. Kristof's intention, he makes clear, is not to pour contempt on anyone's sincere religious devotion. He is simply puzzled and concerned "by the way the great intellectual traditions of Catholic and Protestant churches alike are withering, leaving the scholarly and religious worlds increasingly antagonistic." He worries also because of the conversations he has had with some "self-satisfied and unquestioning" representatives of what we commonly call Islamic fundamentalism. He explains, "The Islamic world is in crisis today in large part because of a similar drift away from [its own] rich intellectual tradition" toward unquestioning, emotional religious fervor. "The heart," Kristof concludes, "is a wonderful organ, but so is the brain."[1]

I share Kristof's concern. As a young person, I became a Presbyterian in large measure *because* of the Reformed movement's conviction that our love of God is somehow incomplete until we love God with our minds, as well as with heart, soul, and strength. But today I worry:

- I worry about what will become of Christian faith—indeed, I worry what will become of the world we live in—if Christians fail to ask the tough, deep, critical, sometimes intractable questions about life. I am concerned about what it will mean for our faith if we choose to ignore life's most profound mysteries and insoluble riddles.
- I am concerned about the integrity of the church if we abandon the curiosity that is unafraid to swim at the deep end of the pool, if we jettison a passion for ideas, for knowledge, and for wisdom for their own sake.
- And I am equally disturbed about what will become of society if persons of faith retreat from the public sphere, where ideas must

fight for their lives among competing interests, where justice is served by vigorous argumentation and intelligent action as much as by high ideals.

Our age is not unique. There have been times in history when knowledge and scholarship were not generally valued. And in some of those times the world's intellectual treasury was preserved by a relative few. We all know the stories, for example, of how tiny cells of Christian monks, in the darkest of the Dark Ages, hid the wisdom of the ancients away for safe-keeping in remote monasteries. But the crisis we face today implicates the church no less than society in general. Today, perhaps more than at any time since the Protestant Reformation, we need to recover that commitment to the life of the mind in the service of God.[2]

If we are determined to recover this commitment, we need to be aware of the forces against which we must contend and the steps we must take to recover in our church a healthy regard for an intellectually rigorous faith, a reasoned faith, a courageous and imaginative faith, a *thinking faith*. Some of the forces arrayed against a thinking faith are not new, though they recently have taken on some new features.

Anyone who has read Arthur Schlesinger's epochal study, *The Age of Jackson*, first published in 1945, knows that the populism that has lent such vitality to American political and social life (and that was inseparable from the Jacksonian revolution in the mid-nineteenth century) has also often manifested an underbelly of anti-intellectualism. This anti-intellectualism, sometimes identified as a rejection of elitism, is particularly evident in certain expressions of Christian faith in our country.[3] Yoked together with the deep strains of individualism and anti-institutionalism that run through American social history, this suspicion of thinking and scholarship—or even of rationality itself—has become almost an article of faith among some American Christians.[4]

This bias against critical thinking is based on assumptions that go so deep into our social psyche and that are so much a part of our culture that many American Christians have never even noticed that they are just that: culturally determined *assumptions* rather than inviolable facts. The anti-intellectualist and anti-institutional forces linked to

American populism have long been with us and have gained traction at particular moments of national insecurity and anxiety. Cultural critics on the right as well as the left have observed this phenomenon.

David Brooks recently described the growth of the newest expression of such populism that, he says, rejects "every single idea associated with the educated class," from global warming to abortion rights, from gun control to multilateral action in foreign affairs.[5] The fact that this populism often reflects a deeply religious, specifically *Christian* identity only compounds the problem facing advocates of a thinking faith.

There are other forces arrayed against a thinking faith, and I would like to elaborate on three in particular: (1) the contemporary cult of superficiality, (2) the insecurity that drives many to demand certainty, and (3) the generalized anxiety of our culture in the face of rapid and far-reaching social and technological change.

The Contemporary Cult of Superficiality

A few years ago, Tom Long, professor of homiletics at the Candler School of Theology at Emory University, observed that the greatest heresy the church faces today is not atheism but superficiality.[6] Tom's thesis may surprise many Christians who view evangelists of atheism like Christopher Hitchens and Richard Dawkins as the supreme threat to faith in our time, but I think Tom is right. In fact, the single greatest antidote to books such as Christopher Hitchens' *God Is Not Great: How Religion Poisons Everything* or Richard Dawkins's *The God Delusion* is not a defensive mode of retrenchment against their ideas, but the rather more ironic response of demonstrating their oversimplification and inadequate critical reflection in relation to their subject matter.[7] Christian scholars have often been far more sophisticated, more searching and self-critical, and at times more scathing in analyzing the problems in Christian faith than either Hitchens or Dawkins. Such scholarship, from the work of Renaissance humanists like Erasmus to that of contemporary scholars such as Luke Timothy Johnson, Margaret P. Aymer, and Brian K. Blount, clears the underbrush of superstition and sloppy thinking so that a more robust faith can grow.

One might go a bit further than Tom Long's assessment, however, to argue that it is the contemporary *cult of superficiality* (and not just superficiality itself) that represents the greatest obstacle to a thinking faith today. I say "cult" because the cultural bias in favor of superficiality takes on so many of the characteristics of a cult, especially the unquestioning ideological loyalty it demands of its adherents and its relentless compulsion to proselytize. The resistance to profundity that dominates so much television news coverage and that characterizes so many marketing schemes is just one aspect of this cult.

Strangely enough, however, it is often the self-appointed guardians of communication and evangelism in the church that represent some of the most strident voices advocating for the cult of superficiality and against deep thinking about our faith. It is hard to imagine how we could, with a straight face, argue that our understanding of God, our relationship with God, and our obligations to live as a people of God should be trivialized and dumbed down—when virtually no one would think it responsible to treat subjects like physics or economics so blithely. And, yet, the publication of books that reduce God-talk to baby-talk proliferates in virtually every Protestant press. The pressure on writers to participate in the cult of superficiality is tremendous, especially for beginning authors who feel they must conform to the ideology of the cult or never see their ideas in print. And pastors across the country know the tyranny of the treadmill fueled by consultants and experts who tell them that they must avoid profound reflection at all costs if they want to attract today's religious market.

Occasionally I hear editors of church publications or church growth consultants arguing that Christian laypeople just aren't interested in theology, or that laypeople aren't interested in the history of their faith or, worse still, that laypeople simply can't understand complicated ideas. Yet, when I speak in congregations around the country, I regularly encounter crowds of lively, intelligent laypeople hungry to know more about their faith. These are laypeople, incidentally, who in their daily lives run businesses and shape economies, teach, read or even write important books on a variety of serious subjects, argue legal cases before judges and juries, write laws that shape our common life, and cure our diseases of the mind and body. These laypeople are tired of being infantilized at church. They want to understand their faith more deeply.[8]

The comments of the laypeople I meet, people who want to learn more about their faith, are often along the lines of what an elderly woman said (once again to Tom Long) one Sunday after he had preached in one of the many congregations in which he speaks around the country. As he was making his way from the pulpit to the sanctuary exit, the woman stepped forward to greet him. Earlier in the evening, Tom had invited members of the congregation to share with him any messages they'd like him to take back to the future ministers he teaches in seminary. As this woman stepped forward, Tom greeted her with the question, "Is there a message you'd like me to take back to the seminary, something you'd like me to tell our students?"

"Yes, there is," she said. "Tell them to take us seriously."

Now, I know that not every person in our churches, or indeed in our society, craves to understand God (or anything else) more deeply. But I would also maintain that at the core of the gospel there is a sacred mandate—we call it "the Great Commission"—to go into all the world to make disciples, "teaching them to obey everything that I have commanded you" (Matt. 28:20). The word *disciple* translates a Greek word that means "pupil" or "willing learner." As church leaders, then, we have this duty, this mission, this commission: *to teach*, to kindle curiosity, to expand knowledge, to renew minds, to make our people wiser. And there are many, many people only too eager to learn.

But please—for just one moment—I want to invite you to be depressed with me.

An episode of *The Jay Leno Show* featured one of those sidewalk interviews for which Leno is so famous. In this one he asked passersby to tell him who lives at "1600 Pennsylvania Avenue."

No one he asked knew the answer.

But in answer to the question, "Who lives in a pineapple under the sea?" everyone he asked knew it was SpongeBob Square Pants.

Now, please understand me: I do not wish to underestimate the significance of any contributions Mr. Square Pants has made to American society or to the world we live in. Nor do I want to belittle the contributions made by fictional cartoon characters as a community, but . . . I'm just saying—good grief! Nobody knew where the

President of the United States lives, but they all knew SpongeBob's address!

We know the forces we face when it comes to the contemporary cult of superficiality, do we not? As a society we celebrate trivial knowledge and devalue informed reflection on core values and traditions, including, for Christians, core values and traditions of our faith. Given this cultural press to celebrate the trivial, as thinking Christians sometimes we have a responsibility to go beyond taking people seriously. We may need to take them more seriously than they take themselves.

Insecurity and the Demand for Certainty

Truth (so the saying goes) is the first casualty of war. But self-criticism is the first casualty of insecurity, especially that insecurity that transforms thinking people into an unthinking herd.

According to one of the leading Christian intellectuals of the last century, Reinhold Niebuhr, "Nations . . . do not easily achieve any degree of self-transcendence, for they have inchoate organs of self-criticism. That is why collective [humanity] always tends to be morally complacent, self-righteous and lacking in a sense of humor."[9] A herd is a herd, whether it sits complacently in front of its television being told what it wants to hear, confirmed in its prejudices, and reinforced in its self-serving ideologies; or whether it stampedes, rushing like a mob from one extreme to another in its search for certainty.

Niebuhr's statement has come to mind often over the past few years as I have watched the taunting, jeering, sometimes frighteningly irrational faces of some of our fellow citizens shouting down elected representatives at so-called town hall meetings. The Christian creed, by contrast, revels in an irony that almost always evokes a smile if not an outburst of self-deprecating laughter. Christian faith thrives on a spirit that resists taking itself too seriously. As G. K. Chesterton fancied, angels can fly because they take themselves lightly. Devils, we might add, fall under the weight of their own self-regard.

The greatest personal confessions of faith often evoke a wry smile. Think, for example, of the confession ascribed (albeit out of context) to Tertullian: "I believe because it is impossible." Or, remember Will

D. Campbell's well-known formulation of the Christian message: "We are all bastards but God loves us anyway."[10] Even those who object to Campbell's language recognize the wisdom contained in his and Tertullian's ironic statements of profound faith. These two make us smile because we recognize in their words not only their sacred truth but also our humanity. They paint the world in subtle shades because they are confident of God's grace.

On the other hand, the mindset of those who are insecure demands—with deadly seriousness—certainty and conformity. The mindset of the insecure denounces irony, ambiguity, and self-criticism as pastimes of the intellectual elite. But irony, ambiguity, and self-criticism are not merely optional accessories of intellectualism; they are (to use a term often used in very different circumstances) fundamentals of faith, because they underscore what Kierkegaard called the "infinite qualitative difference" between us creatures and the Holy One, the eternal Being of Beings.

Reinhold Niebuhr observed the cost of insecurity during the decade following the Second World War. Niebuhr was particularly interested in the ways in which the "religion of Communism," as he described it, was countered by its American opponents. For Niebuhr, Communism represented "a foe the fires of whose hostility are fed by [a] . . . humorless pretension" that "no laughter from heaven could possibly penetrate." But Communism, he said, was being countered by a "frantic" American anti-Communism, the "hatefulness" and "fury" of which was like nothing so much "in spirit" as the Communism it opposed.[11]

There is no doubt that Niebuhr opposed Communism. But Niebuhr's thinking faith (with its sense of humor, its irony, and its self-criticism—all grounded in a healthy appreciation for the tenacity of sin in individuals and institutions) raised the alarm against our becoming spiritually that which we oppose.

A thinking faith is a self-critical faith. A thinking faith knows its own limits because it is guided by a comprehension of a basic reality: we are human. We are creatures. We are not God. Thinking faith's recognition of human finitude generates reverence for transcendence and recognition of the limits even of its own claims.

Thinking faith is characterized as much by its humility and reticence as by its pronouncements. Along with its reverence for God and respect for others, it is characterized by a kind of irreverence toward its own certainty. One might regard thinking faith as a faith chastened by knowledge and experience. One would certainly regard thinking faith as a faith that has made its peace with ambiguity, because it cannot and it will not try to justify itself in the presence of God. But it is inevitable, for these very reasons, for a thinking faith to be thought "weak" by some.[12]

It has become commonplace in our culture for Christians to believe they can only prove their faith by claiming to know the mind of God. Yet, pretensions to certainty do not signal a superabundance of faith. They indicate, rather, faith's vanity and paucity. Religious dogmatism is the child of insecurity. And so Niebuhr, in arguably his most important study, *The Nature and Destiny of Man,* describes how important it is for Christians to try to achieve some degree of that intellectual and spiritual objectivity that always accompanies self-criticism.

"Periodically," Niebuhr says, we would be well advised "to moderate" our "pretensions and admit" that we are only very little animals "living a precarious existence on a second-rate planet, attached to a second-rate sun." This awareness, he says, which cuts the legs from under hubris, is shared with modern scientists who stand dumbfounded in the presence of an unimaginably vast and expanding universe. But, he adds, "it was no modern astronomer who confessed, 'When I consider thy heavens, the work of thy fingers, the moon and the stars, which thou hast ordained: what is [humanity] that thou art mindful of [us]?' (Ps. 8:4)."[13]

As I invited you to be depressed with me earlier, let me now invite you to hope with me. I believe there is reason to hope today that the yearnings for transcendence we see here and there in our culture may well be the one thing that can overcome the pathological demand for certainty.

Recently a fascinating article in the *Chronicle of Higher Education* described a new phenomenon. Students, it said, were coming into university classrooms asking big questions about the meaning of human existence and about their own meaning and purpose — questions that their university professors were unprepared to answer.[14] I am hopeful, not only because the college-bound are asking the "big questions of life," but also because their curiosity is often grounded in their own experiences of serving others, gained in mission opportunities in which they engaged as youth. Increasingly, college students bring into the classroom an awareness of a larger world of need that they have witnessed for themselves, whether in this country or in other parts of the global village. And this awareness is translating into an unwillingness to settle for promises of justice "someday." They do not want to place their concerns for justice on a shelf until they have completed their higher education. That is cause for hope.

Generalized Anxiety in the Face of Rapid Change

It is almost a truism to say that we live in the most anxious of times. A few brushstrokes can paint the background.

- The structures that shape society show stress fractures from top to bottom.
- Institutions, long taken for granted, suddenly are subject to renegotiation.
- The meanings enshrined in basic social frameworks of mutual obligation governing families, marriages, religions, and providing the logic for morality, are hotly contested.
- Hallowed assumptions about the most basic loyalties and allegiances, what it means to be a citizen of a country or a member of a society, even the ordering of such allegiances in relation to one another, are subject to the most radical new questions.
- Innovative technologies are leading to an explosion of previously unimagined information sources, and social media are unsettling long-established spheres of authority and undermining long-respected official sources for reliable knowledge.
- Reports of violence multiply around the globe, often driven by superstition and ignorance.
- Radicalized forces within Western society itself pose a serious threat to internal stability.
- It is a time of unprecedented anxiety.

Oops! I'm so sorry. Apparently I got my notes mixed up. I've just given you my notes summarizing the characteristics of Europe in the years leading to the Protestant Reformation, which I prepared a few months ago for a lecture on the sixteenth century.

Every age believes its time is the most difficult. And it is precisely the perspective provided by a long view of things—a perspective derived from a careful, critical study of history and the ideas and forces that shaped us—that most helps us to face our own challenges. Too easily we forget that history is not the codification of our self-satisfying mythology, but a series of "inquiries." As one historian recently observed of that earliest historian, Herodotus: "When Herodotus . . . began to write down his *Histories*, his Enquiries, he was moved to do it by the enormity of the world-changing events which swirled around the Aegean in his own lifetime."[15]

The best antidote to anxiety is perspective. But anxious people tend to make poor decisions because their anxiety undercuts their ability to gain perspective, to question where they are and how they got there, and to imagine new options based on past experience. Tragically, anxious Christians tend to retrench and become defensive, to draw back, to retreat and to freeze in place at the very moments when they most need to engage their own capacity to be inquisitive and to explore.

Recently some analysts of our culture have described the peculiar variety of cultural anxiety that many are experiencing today as "free-floating anxiety"—that is, an anxiety that is not attached to any specific worry or concern but that floats around and attaches itself first to this issue and then to another. Such "free-floating anxiety," like a virus, is contagious.

If we return to the age of Reformation, we will find among reformers like John Calvin a sense of adventure in the face of the generalized anxiety of their age. Calvin and others embraced the newest information technology—the printing press. Rather than retreating from the wild proliferation of ideas, they encouraged the extension of education. The Protestant reformers founded an astonishing array of new educational institutions for all classes of citizens, preparing the way for the Enlightenment and the scientific revolution that followed. Despite his reputation to the contrary, Calvin and some other reformers actually liberalized deliberative decision-making processes, in ways that led to the birth of modern democratic states. They oversaw the proliferation of new faith communities—the influence of which is felt to this day. Where others constructed roadblocks, Calvin and other reformers imagined opportunities, developing new forms of ministry (particularly in health care and higher education). Along the way they inspired a work ethic that for good reason we call "Calvinist," and a spirit of innovation we term entrepreneurial.

Imagine, if you will, what would have happened to western Europe if the sense of adventure among the reformers had not triumphed over the cultural virus of anxiety: Another Dark Age? Another Bonfire of the Vanities? It could have happened. There's no reason to assume the inevitability of progress. Remember, for a millennium after the fall of Rome we forgot how to mix concrete and how to flush a toilet.

Generalized anxiety, "free-floating anxiety," the dread and panic that ripple through our churches afraid of the future, afraid for their own survival are real factors with which we must contend. They are real barriers to a thinking faith—a dynamic, vital faith.

Again and again we are told that a thinking faith is unpopular, elitist, irrelevant. "It just won't sell in today's market!" But, I would suggest that the best way to deal with all of these barriers is by demonstrating the gift of historical, critical, and creative theological and biblical reflection, by placing the candle of scholarship on a lampstand instead of hiding it under a bushel.

I will give one example. Several years ago it became quite in vogue to say that the mainline church is facing an unprecedented challenge to redefine itself: "the church must change or die." In supporting this argument some reviewed the history of the church and divided its history into three periods: the apostolic period; the Christendom period (now ending); and an unprecedented period lying before us. It was argued that the apostolic period lasted until Christianity became the official religion of the Roman Empire under the emperor Constantine, at which point the age of Christendom dawned. And it is this age, the Christendom age, which is just now disintegrating. We don't know what is going to happen next, because we have had so little experience as a church with different forms of church life. The church has only known two ways of being church in two thousand years! Nobody knows what to do next.[16]

The subsequent comments from our author or church consultant du jour usually went something like this: "Flee! Scurry! Panic! Run for your lives! And do what I say to do, because it's your only hope!"

Now, if you want to guarantee a steady flow of consulting jobs, I would suggest that this is exactly the kind of argument to put forward: simplistic in its vision and capitalizing on society's generalized anxiety so as to induce *more* fear and trembling.

The problem, of course, is that the analysis was woefully inadequate. Indeed its premise was false. The analysis fueled a sense of *crisis*, when what was needed was what Edwin Friedman often referred to as *adventurous leadership.*[17] What was needed even more was a recovery of the gospel of Jesus of Nazareth, because a church preoccupied by its own survival, clinging to its institutional life, is utterly unattractive. It is only in letting go of our lives for Jesus' sake that we can live (Matt. 10:39).

Over the past two thousand years the church has, in fact, passed through scores and scores of different forms of churchly life, not just two. The church has adapted, floundered, thrived, failed, succeeded, fallen, died, and risen again and again. The church has looked like all sorts of things and functioned in all sorts of ways.

For those who know our past, even as we face an uncertain future, our options are many. And the adventure in which we are engaged is suffused with the presence of a God who has always loved freedom more than safety. The church's future depends on this holy and sovereign God, not on us. But one of the things God provides us are minds to remember, to analyze, and to think creatively, so that we can better understand what God is doing and what God requires of us.

Where Are Our Reinhold Niebuhrs?

The barriers to a thinking faith are significant. I would suggest, however, one thing more about them. Perhaps the reason we find it so hard to overcome these barriers is that we haven't really used well the tools at our disposal.

Too often we have trivialized the message of the Christian faith and treated our members like children rather than encouraging and equipping them to engage deeply the profound matters of faith and life. The prevalence of such dumbing down hardly needs further demonstration. Moreover, too often those of us engaged in scholarly pursuits have remained content primarily to publish our findings in jargon-laced academic monographs. We have not felt obligated to discover ways that our subject matter might connect with persons trying to live faithfully in today's world and to make our research accessible to them.

Arrogance is not unknown among those of us who are scholars. Some of us do give the impression that it is below us to communicate with nonspecialists. And it is not unknown for some of us who are willing to communicate with a broader audience to do so in an unengaging or even patronizing manner. But while relevance can become a voracious idol in the cult of superficiality, high scholarly acclaim can also be a false deity, enticing those of us who publish to spend our specialized training and painstakingly honed intellect on abstruse and irrelevant projects. To squander our talents in this way is not merely frivolous; it is failed stewardship, for "from everyone to whom much has been given, much will be required" (Luke 12:48).

What is needed today is a thinking faith in the service of faithful living—intelligence and faith linked together by a commitment to encourage the flourishing of human life and the promotion of justice. What is needed today, as many people have observed, is the kind of thinking that another generation found in people like Reinhold Niebuhr, a theologian who was also a public intellectual. Often our desire for this kind of thinking faith is expressed in the form of a lament—in fact, as a question: "Where are our Reinhold Niebuhrs today?"

I have thought about this question a lot. And I have come to a conclusion: To ask "Where are today's Reinhold Niebuhrs?" may be to misunderstand the moment in which we live and our own culpability in those things that characterize this moment. It may also be that we are overlooking some legitimate heirs to Reinhold Niebuhr among us.

Niebuhrs emerge, at least in part, because we are prepared to listen to them. In fact, Niebuhrs are still among us today, if we would only hear them speak. They seldom speak in sound bites and they are often quite eloquent. They will not answer to the call of our anxieties; in fact, they may ask us to find the courage to tolerate anxiety and to face uncomfortable facts. They will not give us empty promises of certitude, but they can help make life's ambiguities more endurable and perhaps even more fruitful and life-giving.

A few years ago, Garry Wills noted with reference to contemporary leadership that we get the leaders we demand. Maybe we also get the leaders we deserve. But we definitely will not get better leaders unless we demonstrate more responsible followership. "Show me your leader," Wills said, "and you have bared your soul."[18] Perhaps one could say the same regarding our own public intellectuals and theologians—what do our collective choices about which public figures we will heed say about our character?

In the past year, I have asked various audiences and the readership of my blog[19] to suggest candidates for today's Reinhold Niebuhr. I usually primed the pump a bit when I did so by suggesting some candidates of my own.

- When I think of representatives of a thinking faith, my mind immediately goes to Cornel West, whose books *Race Matters* and *Democracy Matters*[20] challenge our assumptions about the most vital social covenants among us and do so from a place of profound Christian faith and deeply human experience.
- When I think about the Reinhold Niebuhrs among us, my mind goes to Marilynne Robinson, who through novels including *Gilead* and *Home* reminds us that some of the most profound questions in life can only be apprehended in narrative form and who in her collection of essays *The Death of Adam* reminds us that other questions, some of which seem very simple, can only be pursued through a carefully structured essay with complex paragraphs.[21]
- When I think of public intellectuals among us, I think of Stephen Prothero, who in his study *Religious Literacy* reminds us that we cannot afford to be ignorant of so important an aspect of contemporary society as religious faith and in his more recent study, *God Is Not One*, helps us understand that our rush to find similarities among faiths can disrespect these religions while a respect for difference can pave the way toward the kind of thoughtful, even reverent, pluralism that might just make it possible for us to live together.[22]

Particularly in responses to my blog, I have received dozens of names suggesting possible contemporary Niebuhrs. What has become clear, however, by the number and variety of respondents to my request is that there is no shortage of people who want and expect leaders to grapple faithfully and thoughtfully with the great issues of our time.

This is why a thinking faith matters so much for us: *In an age* dominated by celebrity worship (and its flipside of envy and contempt for celebrities); *in a time* when we are asked to believe that sordid family squabbles deserve national media coverage while epoch-changing events around the globe are of little consequence to us; *in an era* when a twenty-four-hour news cycle generates an army of fake experts and stokes a pornographic melee of sensationalized trivia; *in a day* when carefully considered judgments and reasoned political discourse give way to self-promotion and demagoguery, and abusive shouting is accorded more weight in the public square than the thoughtful silence that precedes thoughtful response; *in such a time* it is hard to hear through the din and cacophony the voices of a thinking faith or of a faithful reason.

But the voices still remain. And the voices are still valued.

And, for God's sake, for our own sake, and for the sake of the world that God loves we need to find ways to hear these voices, to make room in our congregations for these voices. We need to encourage and cultivate these voices from every pulpit and from every teaching lectern and in every pew and desk in our country.

But there is one thing more that we need: to join our people in the adventure of a thinking faith, because nothing is more crucial to our Reformed project.

Chapter 4

Schism, the Unintended Consequence of the Reformed Project

Among the unfortunate "unintended consequences" of the Protestant Reformation is the tendency of Protestant communities to splinter and split. Tragically the Reformed movement has been particularly susceptible to schism—although our formal theological statements (beginning with those of John Calvin) have consistently placed schism beside heresy as the two greatest sins of which the church can be guilty. We often think of schism in terms of a splitting apart of formal ecclesiastical structures, a polity sin at best. But in reality, schism is a disease of the heart—a sin because it represents a failure to love. Its consequences endure, moreover, because once the bonds of fellowship are eroded, and then broken, subsequent generations are less sure of the basis of their own union. Ever after, the forces to divide compete with unfair advantage against the will to stay together. Schism becomes (to borrow a phrase from Robert Bellah) a "habit of the heart."

An Unhappy Legacy

Back at the very beginning of the Reformed project, John Calvin viewed schism as a violation of the one body of Christ. He was always careful to define the Protestant movement of the sixteenth century as a *reformation* of the church, a return to the church's primitive faithfulness, a recovery of its theological, liturgical, and churchly integrity against a variety of medieval ecclesiastical abuses and corruptions, as we have already observed.[1]

Calvin argued that the Protestant Reformation, while representing a genuinely necessary break from the ecclesiastical structures and various practices of Roman Catholicism, should never be understood as schism— as the splitting apart of the church, or (worse still) as bringing a new church into existence. Such actions would have been anathema to Calvin.

Nevertheless it would be hard to deny that—whatever Calvin's intentions, whatever renewal was kindled throughout Christendom by the Protestant Reformation, and however eloquently and judiciously Calvin drew his distinctions among terms (such as "reformation" and "separation," "schism" and "heresy")—those of us who inherited Calvin's legacy have fallen victim to the very sin he deplored. Schism has remained for centuries an unhappy aspect of the Reformed project that Calvin founded.

Our branch of the Reformation may not deserve to be branded the most schismatic of all the heirs of Protestantism. Surely that distinction goes to the children of the Radical Reformation, the various Anabaptist and other groups that thrived on division. But in contrast to those fellowships (among which the phenomenon we call schism is not necessarily seen as a vice at all), the Reformed family of churches have simultaneously endured a history of contentious church splits while at the same time explicitly portraying schism as a sin.

The dissonance between our convictions as Reformed Christians and our church practices has troubled us for centuries.

We could spend volumes tracing the whole lamented history of the various splits and fragmentations of our Reformed movement, but I am not sure what that would gain for us. Perhaps we would learn more by interrogating this history, by asking it a few questions. In particular, what I want to ask is this:

- Was there something in Calvin's doctrine of the church, in his own theological understanding of what it means to be the church, or maybe something in John Calvin himself that contributed to the tendency toward schism that has plagued (and still plagues) our Reformed project?
- Was there something, perhaps, in the zeitgeist of the Age of Reformation, or perhaps a combination of factors in that era that contributed to the tendency toward schism that has haunted our movement? If so, what were these factors?

• Is there any remedy, theological or otherwise, to our legacy of schism?

I argued earlier that there have been few times in our history when we have so keenly needed a thinking faith. Likewise there have been few times in our history when we have so needed to resist and to find some creative alternative to the spirit of schism that is rending our congregations and national church bodies apart. Some days it seems that every difference of opinion leads to a new division.

Before going further to examine some of the possible roots of the problem of schism and any potential solutions, I should clarify my use of the term "schism."

Difference and Schism

There is and there always has been considerable diversity, difference, and dissonance not only in how Christians understand the Christian message, but in how we live a Christian life—how we engage in the whole "Christian thing," as David Kelsey puts it.[2]

Paul says as much in his first letter to the Corinthians and in Romans. Paul seems to be speaking passionately against those who would split the church apart when he pleads, ". . . there are many members, yet one body. The eye cannot say to the hand, 'I have no need of you,' nor again the head to the feet, 'I have no need of you'" (1 Cor. 12: 20–21). Echoing and expanding on this metaphor, in Romans Paul urges Christians to understand themselves as members of a single body, the body of Christ, through which they are members of one another, and therefore to "love one another with mutual affection," and "outdo one another in showing honor (Rom. 12:4–21). Paul sees such mutual regard and the cultivation of communal harmony as necessary expressions of the transformation and renewal of minds that occurs when believers "present [themselves] as a living sacrifice" to God (Rom. 12:1–2).[3]

Church historians and theologians have discerned divergent, contrasting strains of doctrine, grounded in diverse communities of faith, in the very earliest Christian period.[4] The biblical canon itself represents a multitude of diverse ways of being and living together faithfully as Christians.[5] As I have argued elsewhere, the very titles of the canonical Gospels as we have received them (*According to Matthew, According to Mark, According to Luke, According to John*) signal a variety of "takes" on God's incarnation in Jesus Christ.[6]

What I'm driving at is this: the mere existence of a variety of Christian communities holding different, even conflicting, beliefs and practices does not necessarily indicate a church in schism. It never has. Difference does not equal fragmentation.

From the earliest days of the Christian church there have always been Christian congregations that struggled to understand the Christian-ness of other congregations. For example, the earliest church in Jerusalem apparently never gave up its Jewish observances, while Paul's missionary congregations in Asia Minor represented a whole new (Gentile) way of being Christian, without circumcision or keeping kosher. The diversity of expressions of faith in these various Christian congregations (exemplified in New Testament books like Acts, James, Hebrews, 1 Corinthians, and Galatians) was so profound that, reading the documents today, one sometimes almost feels that the only thing holding the Bible together is its leather cover. Yet, these differences are not equivalent to schism.

As the word is conventionally used, "schism" refers to a "formal and willful separation from the unity of the Church."[7] The word derives from the English transliteration of a Greek word referring to a tear or rent in a piece of cloth, as when Jesus refers to the tear that results when unshrunk cloth is sewed to an old garment (Matt. 9:16). Already in the New Testament era the word was used also to refer to divisions among people because of differing beliefs or aims (as in John 7:43). Application of the term to the church in reference to "a breach in its unity" or a "division of the Church into separated and mutually hostile organizations" follows this early usage.[8] Paul used the term to refer to divisions among the Christians in Corinth (1 Cor. 1:10). But, as J. G. Davies notes, the apostle's "question on that occasion—Is Christ divided?—was answered by a universal negative in the period of the early Church."[9]

From the very outset there is considerable theological tension with regard to the use of the term schism, as Davies continues:

The patristic writers were convinced of two things: first, of the blasphemy and sinful character of schism—hence, according to John Chrysostom, "nothing angers God so much as the division of the Church; even if we have done ten thousand good deeds, those of us who cut up the fullness of the Church will be punished no less than those who cut his body. . . ." And, second, that schism is always outside the Church, i.e., of any two bodies at odds with each other and each asserting itself to be the Church only one of them had the right to the claim.[10]

Davies illustrates the second of his points by reflecting on Augustine's assessment of the Donatist schism (an early schism in the North African Church), observing that although Augustine "had little to object against the Donatists on the grounds of belief," he nonetheless argued "that they were outside the Church since their breach of unity proved their lack of love and therefore of their possession of the Holy Spirit who is its source."[11] Davies concludes his essay with an observation that I think is important for all Christians today, but particularly for those of us engaged in the Reformed project. He writes, "Whatever the causes of schism in the past, and it has to be acknowledged that there may be at times an unfortunate conflict between truth and love, it is difficult not to admit that failure to actualize that unity for which Christ prayed, according to the Fourth Gospel (John 17:21), partakes of the nature of sin which is itself divisive."[12]

Heresy and Schism

Turning our attention again to John Calvin and the very beginning of the Reformed project, we find that it was precisely this concern about the sinfulness of failure to uphold the unity of the church that haunted Calvin as he tried to define his work as a reformer. In Calvin's commentary on 1 Corinthians, he wrote:

It is well known in what sense the fathers used these two terms ["heresy" and "schism"] and what sort of distinction they made between heretics and schismatics. They maintained that heresy consists in disagreement about doctrine; and schism consists rather in an alienation of spirits as, for example, when anyone left the Church because of a grudge he bore, or dislike of the ministers, or inability to get on with others. Despite the fact that bad teaching can only lead to the splitting of the Church, so that heresy is the root and source of schism; and despite the fact that jealousy or pride is the mother of nearly every heresy, it is, nevertheless, a valuable thing to have this distinction between the two.

Thus schisms are to be found either where there are secret animosities, with not a sign of that agreement which there ought to be among believers, or, where conflicting interests are making their presence felt, every one thinking his own way to be right, and having nothing to do with all that the others say or do. Heresies appear when the evil goes so fast and so far that hostility breaks out into the open, and [people] are quite deliberate about dividing themselves up into conflicting groups.[13]

Calvin provides this distinction between schism and heresy in the course of commenting on the passage in 1 Corinthians 11:18–19, the heading for which reads: "When ye come together in the church, I hear there are divisions . . . For there must be also heresies among you." Calvin continues:

[Paul's] reproof here is . . . that they were not in harmony, as Christians ought to be, but in fact everyone was far too much bound up in his own affairs to make the slightest effort to accommodate himself to others. That was the root of that particular abuse. . .; that was the root of their vanity and arrogance, so that each one was putting himself on a pedestal and looking down his nose at others; that was the root of their neglect of edification, and their desecration of the gifts of God.[14]

According to Calvin, both heresy and schism are evil. Calvin attributes them to "the pernicious contrivances of Satan."[15] But they are *distinct* evils.

Heresy relates to false teachings, schism to an alienation of fellowship. Heresy can result from pride, arrogance, self-righteousness, and jealousy and can lead to divisions in the fellowship, but heresy is primarily a matter of doctrine. Schism often results from false teachings; but schism consists in a division of a community into conflicting groups, the forming of conflicting parties and factions. Schism reveals an underlying self-regard that is inconsistent with the humility to which Christ calls his followers. Schism reveals a lack of that quality of love that "is patient . . . kind . . . does not envy . . . does not boast . . . is not proud . . . is not rude . . . is not self-seeking," but "always trusts, always hopes, always perseveres," to echo Paul's great admonition to love, written in response to dissension in the Corinthian church.

Heresy may be described, then, as a transgression against truth. Schism, on the other hand, is a failure to love with that love revealed in Jesus Christ and given by the Spirit of God.

Seen in the best possible light, schism is predicated on the assumption that separation from "unholy" and "unfaithful" coreligionists is necessary to maintain one's own holiness and faithfulness or to preserve the holiness and faithfulness of the church. More often, schism is based on the mistaken view that a lack of respect for others somehow reflects greater reverence for God.

Calvin's rejection of schism as an option for the church conflicts with his actual practice, making him appear ambivalent on the subject. He speaks forcefully against schism, and against the bitterness and brokenness of relationships that are its stock in trade. Calvin rebukes even Reformed colleagues, like John Knox, who appear eager to sacrifice fellowship for the sake of matters that Calvin regards as nonessential.[16] Calvin urges that Christians stand firm against sectarianism. And Calvin does so while engaging in a vigorous, sometimes bitter polemic against what he sees as the false teachings and unfaithful practices of the Roman Catholic Church.

"Breaking Up Is Hard to Do" — or Is It?

Recently I was doing research on a period in Scottish church history from roughly 1750 to 1850. During this era alone I counted at least eight splits among the Reformed churches in Scotland—eight notable breaches of fellowship in about one hundred years.

All but one of these represented breaks from the established Church of Scotland—the church that suffered the mother of all Scottish church schisms in the Great Disruption of 1843, out of which the Free Church of Scotland came into existence. Similar spates of division mar the history of the Reformed churches in Europe and in North America, continuing to threaten the peace and unity of church bodies to this day in the name of purity of faith and practice.

Virtually from the beginning of the Protestant Reformation, we find vital movements fracturing along various fault lines. T. H. L. Parker, in his popular biography of Calvin, observed that by the middle of the sixteenth century the European church had splintered not only into two opposing communions, Roman Catholic and Protestant (or Evangelical, as Protestants are often called in Europe):

> . . . but like some great rock that falls from the cliff and breaks on the boulders below, the evangelicals are not entire. Anglican, Lutheran, Reformed; the charitable titles cover a multitude of dissensions. Lutherans so Lutheran that they make the young Martin Luther look like the pope, savage the moderate Lutherans whom they call crypto-Calvinists. Zürich, faithful to its warrior-theologian, distrustful of Geneva; Bern . . . calling down fire from heaven on the writings of Calvin. And in England they are measuring out the ground for the duels of the next reign.[17]

We have already said that while John Calvin deplored schism and thought it evil, the Reformed or Calvinist branch of the Reformation has been as subject to schism as any other. Parker carefully documents this observation. In the *Institutes,* Calvin affirmed the unity of the Church, writing unequivocally:

> The church is called "catholic," or "universal," *because there could not be two or three churches unless Christ be torn asunder—which cannot happen!* But all the elect are so united in Christ that they are dependent on one Head, they also grow together into one body, being joined and knit together as are the limbs of a body. They are made truly one since they live together in one faith, hope, and love, and in the same Spirit of God. For they have been called not only into the same inheritance of eternal life but also to participate in one God and Christ. Although the melancholy desolation which confronts us on every side may cry that no remnant of the church is left, let us know that Christ's death is fruitful, and that God miraculously keeps his church as in hiding places.[18]

Parker comments on Calvin's words:

> This unity is unity within the one Christ. The foundation of the
> church is [remember this phrase!] *the election of individuals. . . .*
> The concept of unity is at the very heart of Calvin's doctrine of
> the church. It has been said that Calvin's thinking is collectivist
> throughout. Better to say [his thinking is] unitive. . . . He regarded
> nothing so unchristian, ungodly, and against the true order of
> things as disunity.[19]

Having described the rich "unitive" center of Calvin's understanding of the church, Parker then asks the obvious question as
to why Calvin left the Roman Catholic Church if he believed so
deeply that the church is one. "Precisely," Parker writes, "because he
regarded this institution as no longer the church of God."[20] Indeed,
Calvin argued that it was necessary to "withdraw" from fellowship
with Rome "that we might come to Christ."[21] The Reformed project
sought to restore the church that had been so desecrated as to have
been lost.

Calvin's argument is carefully nuanced. Calvin tried to hold in
tension the fundamental and objective reality of the church's unity in
Jesus Christ, and the vagaries and divisions among us in our struggles
to be faithful. Calvin believed that the church ultimately is a spiritual
reality made up of the elect known to God alone. The church, in this
sense, is visible to God but is hidden from the world. Only God can
judge truly who is among its membership. Thus François Wendel, in
his excellent biography of Calvin, writes:

> It is not, therefore, by the quality of its members which could only
> give occasion for a subjective judgment, but by the presence of the
> means of grace instituted by Christ, that the Church is constituted
> and can be objectively judged. Calvin was well aware . . . that
> there could be no question of forming an ideal human community
> composed of the righteous and the saintly, such as the Anabaptists
> desired, for instance. Seeing that we cannot clearly distinguish the
> righteous from the reprobate and that Christians themselves remain
> sinners throughout their earthly life, it would be presumptuous and
> practically impossible for access to the Church to be restricted to
> the perfect alone. Taking up an idea that he had expressed . . . in
> 1536, Calvin concludes that by a "charitable judgment" all may

properly be held to be members of the Church who, by their faith, their conduct and their participation in the sacraments "confess one same God and one same Christ with us." Conversely we have to constitute the Church by basing ourselves upon our communion with Christ, and manifesting the same outwardly in the preaching of the Gospel and the administration of the sacraments.[22]

While maintaining the conviction that ultimately the church *as a spiritual reality* is visible only to God, Calvin felt compelled to say that the church's authenticity and integrity are to some degree discernible in history. There are times and places, in other words, where the visible institution we call the church and the invisible church "overlap," as my friend David Johnson has observed. Though the visible church "is strictly temporal," and though the church is a fallen creature, frail, fragile and wounded, Johnson says, it is nonetheless "the custodian of the Word, the proclaimer of the Word, and the obedient child of the Word."[23]

John Calvin regarded as the "true Church" the church that faithfully proclaims the Word of God and rightly administers the sacraments. Conversely, according to Calvin, a religious body, nominally Christian, however holy its pretensions, however ancient its traditions, if it is corrupt in its ecclesiastical practices, if it does not faithfully proclaim the Word of God and does not properly administer the sacraments, cannot legitimately be called the church. There is a point of frailty, fragility, woundedness, corruption, beyond which the visible church cannot go and still be regarded as true church—a point at which one can no longer have confidence in it, and it may be regarded as false or dead.

Calvin's understanding of the church holds in tension, *first,* that "there must always be a church in the world" and, *second,* that a church can become so utterly false, its doctrines so ruined and sacraments so desecrated, that it can die. Thus, even as Calvin makes his case for the corruption of the Roman Church, he takes care to report the voices of those whose witness gives evidence to the persistence of the true Church of Jesus Christ in history (the "hidden seed" that God preserves) even in the Roman Church.[24]

It is at this point, however, that a phrase with so much potential for Calvin, the phrase "charitable judgment," cannot sustain the weight he places upon it. Love is tested to the breaking point by the apparent necessity and compulsion to make judgments with reference to the faith of others within the veil of history.

Calvin is at pains to make crucial distinctions here. He writes: "[W]hen we categorically deny to the papists the title of *the* church, we do not for this reason impugn the existence of churches among them. Rather, we are only contending about the true and lawful constitution of the church, required in the communion not only of the sacraments . . . but also especially of doctrine."[25]

Surveying the European constellation of Christianity, Calvin initially draws back from a comprehensive judgment against the Roman Church. His invectives against the pope are unrelenting. Calvin declares the pope to be "the leader and standard bearer of that wicked and abominable kingdom," but Calvin also refuses to deny that there are churches "under his tyranny" that are and remain true church.[26] *However,* while Calvin strives to maintain his own "charitable judgment" toward Roman Catholicism, his rhetoric soon turns bitter. He writes:

> But these [churches that remain true] he [the Pope] has profaned by his sacrilegious impiety, afflicted by his inhuman domination, corrupted and well-nigh killed by his evil and deadly doctrines, which are like poisoned drinks. In them Christ lies hidden, half buried, the gospel overthrown, piety scattered, the worship of God nearly wiped out. In them, briefly, everything is so confused that there we see the face of Babylon rather than of the Holy City of God. To sum up, I call them churches to the extent that the Lord wonderfully preserves in them a remnant of his people, however woefully dispersed and scattered, and to the extent that some marks of the church remain—especially those marks whose effectiveness neither the devil's wiles nor human depravity can destroy. But on the other hand, because in them those marks have been erased to which we should pay particular regard in this discourse, I say that every one of their congregations and their whole body lack the lawful form of the church.[27]

In a torrent of first person *singular* lamentation and wrath (in contrast to his earlier, more measured, first person *plural* theological arguments), Calvin talks himself out of his moderate position; he abandons his own "charitable judgment" as though to say: "I take it all back! Root and branch, it's all false! There is no church left in *that* church!"

John Calvin's most relentless opponent in debate turns out to be John Calvin! Rationality clashes with passion. Theology conflicts with bitter experience. Respect for the sovereign providence, the eternal wisdom and judgment of God rages against the all-too-human need to know, to judge between true and false, righteous and unrighteous, good and evil. The grace that leaves to God what only God can comprehend struggles against the experience of a man who has seen for himself the fruits of corruption in church and feudal court.

Calvin's Reformed heirs inherit the full legacy of a schism within John Calvin's own heart, and within his theology. And, soon, as the historical crow flies at least, Calvin's heirs turned inward the full force of his schismatic legacy. They turned upon their own Reformed movement the relentless, divisive spirit that judges others whatever the consequences may be for Christian love.

The lesson seems to be that once we have a theological rationale that gives us permission to split our fellowship, we will inevitably split. For Calvin, the object of scrutiny was the Roman Catholic Church, which he seemed to believe must be pronounced dead to justify the birth of the Reformed movement. For Calvin's heirs, the object of scrutiny became the Reformed communion itself. The anathemas have not yet ceased to fly.

There is something else, something perhaps more difficult to define as either theological or personal, but which is distinctive when Calvin's argument turns from the critical, but measured plural "we" statements to his harsh, bitter and often unqualified personal "I" pronouncements. Previous medieval-era reform and renewal movements within the Catholic Church allowed for diversity within a larger ecclesiastical framework, thus preserving unity. Calvin and various Protestant reformers' assertion of individual judgment over the prerogative of such churchly incorporation of renewal movements represented an essential departure from those previous movements.

The centrifugal forces of individualism, or perhaps more accurately, the disintegrating forces of "the individual self," which are distinctive in the Protestant Reformation, contribute to this tendency of the magisterial "I" to excommunicate others whose faith and practices differ from "mine." This continues to haunt Protestantism and the Reformed movement to this day.

This centrifugal force toward disintegration only increased after the original generations of reformers (from Luther to Calvin) exited the stage of history, and as their successors wrangled over their relative status and power, and as these successors attempted to solidify the gains of the Reformed project by converting an essentially evangelical movement into an impregnable ecclesiastical fortress. Ironically, the well-documented retrenchment of scholastic Calvinism undermined the centripetal forces that would have made it possible for the center to hold.[28]

The particular version of individualism implicit in the Protestant Reformation and the variety of its causes and implications has been explored by many theologians, philosophers, historians, and sociologists.[29] Recently, for example, James Simpson, a professor of English at Harvard University, observed the destructive individualistic forces that are inseparable from a kind of Protestant mythology of the reader's unmediated relationship to the biblical text, an approach that, in the evangelical traditions (such as Calvinism), undercuts community and inevitably tends toward schism.[30]

The ambivalence toward tradition—indeed, the sometimes aggressive hostility in reaction to the very notion of tradition—has its corollary in a tendency to elevate, and to view as theologically heroic, the ideal of the isolated reader in contrast to any communal or churchly mediation of the biblical text. This ambivalence and certainly this hostility provide fertile ground for schism—despite the fact that we may see in this ambivalence a number of positive aspects.[31]

There is something else in the schism one witnesses in the Protestant Reformation, something at once very human but also potentially dehumanizing. Schism is not so much an act of institutional or even communal separation as it is a disposition of the heart. Schism is a spiritual disease.

John Calvin knew this, and this is, at least in part, why he feared so deeply the forces of schism. Schism represents an act of judgment based on an assumption of moral or religious superiority and spiritual self-justification. It is the bitterness of the personal invective that fully manifests schism, not the official pronouncements and acts of parliaments, church councils, or popes.

Understanding schism in this light, it seems obvious why Calvin's personal asides are more divisive than his carefully modulated theological reflections, even when these reflections describe abuses that he believes must be addressed critically. The spirit of schism, with its bitterness and invectives, judgment and hatred, represents a persistent undercurrent in the Protestant Reformation, breaking through *especially* in the letters and personal comments of reformers: sometimes in sarcasm, sometimes in lamentation, sometimes in fiery wrath. But, it must also be said, the spirit of schism resided in the heart of Rome no less than in the hearts of the Protestant reformers, and is evidenced in the manner in which retaliation was unleashed.

Calvin's dilemma should not be caricatured. It represented a fundamental and legitimate struggle that, given the realities in church and society in his time, was all but inevitable. But once the genie of schism escaped the bottle, once all the crumbs were shaken from the bottom of Pandora's mixed bag, we could scarcely avoid the consequences of continuing schism (and I mean by this a continuing spirit of schism, of bitterness and judgment) within and among the communities that make up the Reformed movement itself.

This is not simply a theological tale, and the answers we seek run like tendrils through the historical period in which the Protestant Reformation occurred. Schism caught fire in the sixteenth century for reasons other than merely theological and ecclesiastical. Something shifted in the sense of self. Calvin was not the only "I" speaking with new authority. And that "something" that shifted had technological, cultural, social, political, and philosophical *as well as* ecclesiastical elements.

Looking to the Doctrine of Christ
to Correct our Doctrine of the Church

From a theological perspective, it is especially lamentable that schism became lodged in the Reformed movement. This need not have been the case.

Coveting is to theft what schism is to the divisions of the church. Schism is the heart of the sin that leads to the breach of fellowship. Once schism occurs in our hearts, everything else—from the interminable squabbles among neighbors to civil litigation—is analogous to the nasty business of a divorce settlement once a marriage has been abandoned. Schism is a sin because it represents a failure to love. Moreover, its consequences endure long after the breach of fellowship, because once the bonds of fellowship are eroded and then broken, subsequent generations are less sure of the basis of their own union; ever after, the forces to divide compete with unfair advantage against the will to stay together. Schism becomes (to borrow a phrase made famous by Robert Bellah et al.) a "habit of the heart."[32]

Although the factors that pushed Calvin toward schism were shared with the larger culture in which Calvin lived, Calvin himself *did* contribute to the problem. Yet he also, at least potentially, pointed toward a solution, though there was a self-limiting factor in his theology that undercut this solution.

In Calvin's discussion of "sanctification," he accomplished what he was not able to accomplish in his doctrine of the church, and he did it because of his firm belief (as he himself says in his commentary on the Epistle to the Colossians) "that all things are in Christ, and that [Christ] alone ought to be sufficient and more than sufficient."[33]

Calvin's understanding of our salvation directs our attention away from the individual, away from our righteousness, away from our faith, away from what we might call our "religious experience." Calvin focuses our attention on Jesus Christ, "the mirror of our sanctification," in whom alone we can see our humanity in its wholeness. Calvin writes in his commentary on Ephesians (on 1:20):

> Christ alone . . . is the mirror in which we can contemplate that which the weakness of the cross obscures in us. When our minds are roused to trust in righteousness, salvation, and glory, let us learn to turn them to Christ. We still lie under the power of death; but He, raised from the dead by heavenly power, has the dominion of life. We struggle under the bondage of sin, and, surrounded by endless miseries, we fight a hard warfare, but He, sitting at the right hand of the Father, obtains the highest government in heaven and earth, and triumphs gloriously . . . For these reasons, it is to our good to transfer our thoughts to Christ, that in Him, as in a mirror, we may see the glorious treasures of Divine grace, and the immeasurable greatness of the power which has not yet been manifested in ourselves.[34]

For Calvin, as Trevor Hart has said, "Imputation . . . is not a matter of fiction, but a real sharing or fellowship in the righteousness of" Jesus Christ. "It is, first and foremost, external to us, yet it really belongs to us because of the union which we have with" Christ.[35]

Calvin wanted to remove our doctrine of the church away from the subjectivism that he knew tended to schism. His understanding of salvation points toward the solution that his doctrine of the church never achieved. He was rightly worried about the centrifugal forces of division let loose in the Reformation. When our attention shifts from the union the church is given in Jesus Christ to any other ground for union (whether in some aspect of our doctrine or our practice) then the church's union is inevitably rendered subjective and unsure. Of all the things Calvin taught—if our concern is to reflect in our common life the activity of the Holy Spirit who is the living bond of love and peace in the triune God—it is this we must remember: union with Jesus Christ is our only ground for union with one another. But this is where the problem lies for Calvin's theology, is it not?

The weak link in Calvin's doctrine of salvation, and consequently in his doctrine of the church, is his doctrine of election. According to Calvin, the invisible church is a spiritual reality consisting of elect individuals joined together. While Calvin wished to shift our attention to Jesus Christ and away from ourselves, in fact, his doctrine of election inevitably turns our gaze back to the individual as the prime site of concern. It is this that ultimately undercuts Calvin's "unitive" instincts, as it also tragically undermines the individual's assurance of election. Once again, we see the wisdom of Ernst Käsemann's warning (noted in chapter 2) about allowing anything, even the doctrine of the church, to dominate our vision.[36]

Reformed theology would wait centuries to slice through this Gordian knot, until Karl Barth's remarkable christological interpretation of election. Barth's doctrine of election understands Jesus Christ as the "electing God" *and* the one whom God elects for us, supplying precisely that which Calvin's theology needed.[37] In fact, Barth, in his superb critique of Calvin, asks how "even the Word of God" can give us assurance of our election "if Jesus Christ is not really the electing God, not the election itself, not our election, but only an elected means whereby the electing

God . . . executes that which [God] has decreed concerning those whom [God] has—elsewhere and in some other way—elected?"[38] In other words, when we speak of our being elected by God, we are saying that when God looks at us God sees Jesus Christ in our place. God accepts us fully and forever in Jesus Christ. God does not merely use Jesus Christ as a means to redeem a group of people God chose in some secret manner apart from God's incarnation in Christ. When we have seen Jesus Christ, we have looked into the heart of God. And we see there our inclusion in God's redemptive will for humanity, which is identical with God's full revelation in Jesus Christ.

Barth argues that not only did Calvin not answer the crucial question, but Calvin did not even perceive its significance. Calvin could not have anticipated that this "is the decisive objection which we have to bring against his whole doctrine of predestination."[39]

Barth's judgment on Calvin is only partially right, however. Calvin's doctrine of salvation itself calls for Barth's understanding of election because of the prominence Calvin gives to the high priesthood of Jesus Christ—an understanding of Christ that potentially could have provided Calvin the essential unitive center of our salvation and our life together as church in the person and work of Jesus Christ. The high priesthood of Christ directs our attention away from the subjective vagaries of our individual experiences and responses and attempts at faith and righteousness, toward the objective act of God on our behalf (in and through Jesus Christ, our heavenly high priest), so providing an inner guard against the spirit of schism in the church.[40]

Jesus Christ, our heavenly high priest, holds us together. Jesus Christ, our heavenly high psriest bears us (as church, as individuals) in himself, and brings us in himself into the very life of God. We are one in him. We are only one in him. We have no other unity but in Jesus Christ. This act of unity who is Jesus Christ is God's doing, not ours. Jesus Christ is our peace—the author, pioneer and finisher of our faith, who has faith for us, on our behalf. In Jesus Christ alone is our election sure, because he is the electing God and he is our election. Jesus Christ is our righteousness; even as he became sin for us, he embodies the fullness of righteousness on our behalf. Jesus Christ is the mirror of our unity, no less than of our reconciliation, redemption, and sanctification, because only in Jesus Christ is our faith, our prayer, our worship, our practice, our purity, our life together, made real and whole. This is the objective fact we are called in Christ to apprehend by faith.

The seeds of schism do lie in Calvin's ecclesiology, and they lie also at the root of our Reformed project. There's no denying this. We have harvested their bitter fruit again and again in our history. But, at least potentially, the seeds for understanding our unity in Jesus Christ also lie in Calvin's theology, and they may yet render in us a more "charitable judgment" of those with whom we differ.

Chapter 5

Wonder, Spiritual Transformation, and Reformed Worship

People want congregations to place the expectancy of a transforming experience of God at the heart of the community's life, worship, and mission. To address this yearning with faith and theological integrity, we must discover in our history and our own encounters with God how to teach our people to be attentive to the presence of the "sacred other," the living God, who alone transforms us and gives our lives eternal significance. If we try to manufacture experiences of God's presence, we will give a counterfeit coin of our own minting in place of the genuine currency. Our task is to serve as docents, or ushers, in the house of wonder: escorting our people with humility, respect, and reverence to the threshold of the holy, and opening doors to awareness of the presence of God in all of life. We set the conditions for apprehension of the mystery.

What People Want: Encounter with the Living God

Sometimes it turns out that a book we may not particularly like makes a really important point. One such book, for me at least, was Donald Miller's *Reinventing American Protestantism*, a resource that has been widely read by pastors, academics, and a variety of church leaders since its publication in 1997.[1]

Miller, a professor of religion at the University of Southern California, borrows categories from marketing and sociology to argue for the viability of what he calls "new paradigm churches," such as

Calvary Chapel and the Vineyard. It is tempting to critique the weaknesses of this book, and in my view there are some.[2] However, I want to focus on a positive feature of Miller's argument that makes it impossible to dismiss his book out of hand.

People in contemporary North American society, Miller argues, are yearning for a "transcendent experience of the sacred" that conveys "the self-transcending and life-changing core of all true religion."[3] According to Miller, people want to participate in congregations that place the expectancy of a transforming experience of God at the heart of the community's life, worship, and mission. I believe Miller is right about this. I also believe that this desire and this expectancy are at the heart of our Reformed project. But the prospect of such transforming experiences is both promising and threatening to those traditions of mainline Protestant Christianity that have tended to emphasize Christian formation at the expense of spiritual transformation.

The term "transformation" is slippery in contemporary usage. For the purposes of this chapter, I will stay close to the sense conveyed in two Pauline texts:

- "And all of us, with unveiled faces, seeing the glory of the Lord as though reflected in a mirror, are being transformed into the same image from one degree of glory to another; for this comes from the Lord, the Spirit." (2 Cor. 3:18)
- "I appeal to you therefore, brothers and sisters, by the mercies of God, to present your bodies as a living sacrifice, holy and acceptable to God, which is your spiritual worship. Do not be conformed to this world, but be transformed by the renewing of your minds, so that you may discern what is the will of God—what is good and acceptable and perfect." (Rom. 12:1–2)

In both of these passages the word "transform" is derived from a Greek word we usually transliterate into English as "metamorphose." This word is used in Matthew 17:2 and Mark 9:2 to speak of a visible, outward change in Jesus, who was *transfigured* into his heavenly glory. In both of the above passages from Paul, however, the "change" or "metamorphosis" is "invisible to the physical eye."[4]

Paul apparently views this metamorphosis as more than merely a change in behaviors or habits—though indeed, both behaviors and habits (and any number of other personal factors such as emotions and affections) may be influenced or altered by spiritual transformation.[5] Rather, he views transformation primarily as a cognitive change. It is a change related to people's knowledge of and participation in God's Word and Spirit, a change grounded in God's own being and acting, a change that may resist or oppose certain other influences on people's lives. Krister Stendahl explains that in Romans 12, where Paul reflects on the character of spiritual transformation, "there is, more than in any other passage in Paul that I know, an abundance of words for the mind, for thinking, for what we would call 'brain activities.'. . . 'Transformed in our minds' does not mean that we should not use our minds. They are renewed minds."[6]

Stendahl is here alluding to a tension in Christian faith that has been particularly evident among those of us engaged in the Reformed project, a tension just as persistent as the one I noted in the last chapter between our consistent rejection of schism and our commission of it. But in this instance, the tension Stendahl observes is potentially creative, involving as it does two vital components of the spiritual life: on the one hand the life of the (thinking) mind in the service of God, and on the other hand those supra-rational, even irrational experiences that express the affective dimensions of the Spirit. Both of these are aspects of spiritual transformation, a "transcendent experience of the sacred."[7]

One need only survey American church history from the eighteenth century's controversies over the First Great Awakening to the breathtaking schism that occurred in Presbyterianism in the 1920s to discern the recurring anxieties among mainline Protestant churches in the face of emotionalism and irrationalism—qualities that are sometimes associated with "transformational" or "conversion" experiences, but which are potentially disruptive to the status quo.[8] Yet, these same traditions, in common with Christian churches throughout the world, especially Pentecostal churches in the United States and churches of the Global South, also enshrine in their worship, theology, and polity a reverence for the transcendence, holiness, and freedom and sovereignty of God, in whose presence all churchly control over religious experience is shown to be provisional and relative. While the history of mainline Protestant denominations demonstrates a persistent concern about emotionalism and irrationalism (and the ways charismatic Christian preachers use both to manipulate their followers), the reverence for the holy exhibited in these denominations also conveys their deep respect for the possibility of genuine spiritual transformation in Christians' lives. We forget or ignore this possibility at our own peril.

A tension between the Spirit's engagement of Christians' thinking minds and its affective or supra-rational working has characterized church life from the very beginning. Paul addresses the tension at length in 1 Corinthians 14. At least some among the Corinthians have been priding themselves on the uninhibited way the Spirit manifests itself in their worship services, especially through their exercising of the gift of glossolalia—speaking in tongues, a gift in which the rational mind is disengaged (1 Cor. 14:14). Paul, too, treasures this particular expression of the Spirit's presence, claiming that he practices tongue-speaking even more often than they do. But he regards their worship services as free-for-alls, and insists that they institute a measure of order and decorum. Tongues should be accompanied by *interpretation* and by *prophecy* (which Paul views as expressions of the rational mind: see vv. 15, 18–19), and all must take turns (see vv. 26–33a). The envisioned orderliness will serve to build up the church. Indeed, Paul sees it as a way of expressing that love for God and one another for which he advocated so beautifully a few lines earlier, in 1 Corinthians 13. Moreover, the decorum serves an evangelistic purpose: the outsider who witnesses the Spirit-filled congregation worshiping "decently and in order" will be convicted, find the secrets of her heart disclosed, and fall down before God, declaring, "God is really among you" (1 Cor. 14:25).[9] Yet, even the properly ordered worship that Paul pictures would scarcely have been a staid and routine affair. He presumes the Spirit's lively and unpredictable intervention in the community's midst: freely dispensing hymns, revelations, tongues, and interpretations among participants.

There are two additional tensions connected with spiritual transformation in the Reformed tradition that must be mentioned here. The first is the tension between the individual quest for spirituality and spirituality as a communal venture (discussed in chapter two). The second is a tension between experience of the sacred that remains set apart from ordinary life and spirituality that is embedded in the ordinary. My colleague Susan Garrett explored this tension in her book, *No Ordinary Angel: Celestial Spirits and Christian Claims about Jesus*, reflecting on sets of comments by journalist Marta Vogel and scholar Laurie Zoloth-Dorfman.[10]

Vogel tells the story of her own "search for a church that would satisfy her craving for sacred moments." Her autobiographical remarks could serve as sound bites for Donald Miller's thesis. In a conversation with her husband Vogel says, "I want to lose myself, to not be able to think about whether Cheerios are on sale at the grocery store or whether I need to call the plumber to fix the downstairs bathroom."[11] Garrett observes that Vogel "was looking for a time each week set apart from the mundane, a time that would shift the balance of her life so that she was not so much 'of the world.' She was looking, she writes, 'to feel a lump in my throat, a swelling in my chest.'"[12] Zoloth-Dorfman, by contrast, critiques the long-standing view of spirituality in which genuine spiritual experience occurs only as a solitary quest, in "sacred time" and "sacred space." Writing especially out of her own and others' experience as women (who, like Vogel, have so often had to be preoccupied with the ordinary and mundane), Zoloth-Dorfman advocates for a pursuit of the sacred, not apart from but *in and through* the everyday, a recovery of the holiness of the mundane moment and the ordinary place.[13]

Each of these tensions, to one degree or another, provides energy for the arguments surrounding spirituality in Protestant churches today, including arguments about so-called traditional versus contemporary worship. Sometimes the tensions are latent, their significance invisible even to protagonists locked in disputes, but at other times the tensions break out with fierce urgency and are spoken in the most derisive and abusive terms. Sadly, we can become so bogged down in our arguments that we overlook the extraordinary good news that should fill us with hope.

Many people are coming to church today, Don Miller and others are telling us, seeking a profound, life-changing encounter with God. If they are correct—and I believe they are—what are the implications of this good news for congregations and congregational leaders who would like to reform our churches so that they can become sites of transformation? What might it mean for us to assume the task of ushering our congregants into spiritually transforming experiences through worship and preaching, counseling, and congregational leadership?

In order to address these questions, in the next section I will explore one approach to thinking about pastoral ministry and the leadership of congregations that has proven especially influential in North America during the past fifty years. Then I will describe how we must embrace, yet go beyond this way of thinking in order to engage persons at the level of their longing for transformation.

The Fourth Perspective on Ministry

Seward Hiltner mapped the terrain of congregational ministry for a generation in his watershed study, *Preface to Pastoral Theology: The Ministry and Theory of Shepherding*.[14] In this book, which became the textbook (literally) for the next two or three generations of seminarians, he described three perspectives on ministry, particularly ministry led or organized by pastors and other official congregational leaders. These perspectives are *communicating, organizing*, and *shepherding*. Whatever the various acts or "operations" (as Hiltner called them) of pastoral ministry in which one is involved, each of these perspectives plays its distinctive role: coloring, shaping, qualifying, limiting, and defining how pastors and other church leaders carry out their tasks. The act ("operation") of preaching, for example, may reflect any or all of these perspectives at any given time. Preaching typically is understood to reflect the perspective of *communicating* the claim of the Word of God on "the minds and hearts and lives of people."[15] Preaching can, however, reflect the perspective of *shepherding*—what Hiltner describes as the "readiness of the shepherd to be attentive" to hearers whenever "they need or wish tender and solicitous concern."[16] Preaching may also reflect the perspective of *organizing,* that is, the concern of those responsible for congregational leadership to deepen and extend the social embodiment of the church as the "Body of Christ" through the ordering and administrating of the church's ministry.[17]

Hiltner's assertion that preaching can manifest all three perspectives—communicating, shepherding, organizing—applies also to any number of other "operations" of ministry, from the leadership of worship to the moderation of church boards, from teaching a confirmation class to providing pastoral counseling. The three perspectives are in fact deeply interrelated. As we practice pastoral ministry, and as we are mindful of these three perspectives, we are able to discern the organic wholeness of ministry, in contrast to approaches that tend to fragment ministry into various technical or professional specializations. The *communication* of the gospel cannot be divorced from *shepherding* persons, except at the risk of doing real harm both to the gospel and to those who hear its message. The *organization* of a congregation cannot be understood in isolation from the perspectives of *communicating* the gospel and *shepherding* persons, without losing the meaning of the church itself as people of God called to follow Jesus Christ. What Hiltner has identified as "perspectives" are, indeed, tightly interrelated concerns running throughout the history of Christianity.[18]

A pastor communicates the gospel, and the gospel makes its claim on the hearts of hearers, whether the pastor teaches adults in a Bible study or engages in a long-range planning process with the congregation's official leadership. The pastor participates in organizing, administrating, and leading the congregation, whether he or she is standing behind the Lord's Table or seated in the moderator's chair of a church board. The pastor shepherds the flock and serves as a physician of the soul through all sorts of practices of ministry, which contribute to the healing, health, and wholeness of the people of God, individually and collectively.

Each of Hiltner's perspectives has biblical, theological, and historical warrants, and each has limitations. The classical doctrine of Christ's threefold office as prophet, priest, and king (emphasized in certain streams of Reformed faith, including Calvin) reflects these perspectives. Scholarly studies of the historical and contemporary models of pastoral ministry, such as David Bartlett's *Ministry in the New Testament*, Donald Messer's *Contemporary Images of Christian Ministry*, and Avery Dulles's *Models of the Church* elaborate on this simple pattern.[19] Even attempts to reduce pastoral ministry to salesmanship, marketing, and customer service implicitly seek the authority conveyed in these perspectives. And it is ultimately in light of these deeply grounded perspectives of communicating, organizing, and shepherding that such *mis*understandings of pastoral ministry must be judged as theologically inadequate.

What has sometimes been neglected, however—or simply lost in the shuffle of our conversations about the exercise of pastoral ministry and church leadership—is the essential theological "perspective" of *awe and reverence in the presence of the holy*. Hiltner assumed the underlying existence and importance of this fourth, *theological* perspective, which undergirds everything else we have to say about ministry. He alluded to it when he warned of the danger of "minimizing the difference between saving knowledge and other knowledge" and thus winding-up in pastoral ministry "with a humanism that has forgotten the awe and majesty and transcendence of God and the overwhelming and ultimate significance of Jesus Christ."[20]

Without reference to this radical ("radical" in the sense of the "root") perspective of divine encounter, we run the risk of losing altogether the spiritual significance of pastoral ministry, pastoral care, congregational leadership, our service to one another and the world, our ministries of justice, and our vital witness as disciples of Jesus Christ. Without reference to this basic theological perspective of reverence in the presence of God, ministry (particularly ordained ministry) can collapse in upon itself as an earnest but hopelessly self-referential and personally exhausting professionalism. Without explicit reference to this underlying perspective of sacred awe, our fears of the *excesses* of emotionalism and irrationalism can all too easily be translated into institutional barriers to *the very possibility* of personal transformation by the power of the Holy Spirit.

What I propose is this: a recovery in pastoral ministry and congregational leadership of the radical perspective of reverence in the presence of the sacred Other, and a recovery of the defining identity of all who minister (both lay and ordained) as what I will call *docents in the house of wonder*. (I will define and describe this phrase in the following section.) I ask that we reconceive our ministry as a ministry of transformation—seeing ourselves as humble guides into the mysteries of God, as servants who lead among and on behalf of a people of God, assisting others in becoming theologically conscious of the God who, though closer to us than we are to ourselves, never ceases to be wholly and entirely God.

"Immanence," as a theological concept, then, is not an abstract quality, but is none other than the presence of the transcendent God—God who is not only *other* but *wholly* other, God who is free to judge and to grace and thereby to remake us. The vocation of those who minister is to call others into the presence of this holy and transforming God, and to do so in all of life. In carrying out this vocation, we will find again the only power that matters for ministry—the power that can deliver our congregations from captivity to the idol of consumerism and us as leaders from idolatrous consumption of the latest gimmicks or sociologically "relevant" theories du jour, which threaten to render the church utterly irrelevant.[21] Through the exercise of this vocation, we will reclaim the integrity of the spiritual life as we help others to recognize God's sovereignty over both the public and the private dimensions of our lives, to affirm the responsibility of the individual subject within the life of the community, and to rediscover the torn veil that admits us to the Holy of Holies even in the mundane moments of our existence.

Neither the church nor its theologians have ever disowned the radical theological perspective on encounter with God that underlies the three perspectives of pastoral ministry described by Hiltner. But we have, from time to time, ignored the explicitly theological fourth perspective of sacred reverence and have done so to the detriment of the church and society. In a sense, I am asking us to remember Calvin's insight to which I have alluded indirectly: "*In tota vita negotium cum Deo*" ("in all of life it is with God that we have our dealings").[22] The various sociological, psychological, cultural, political, and linguistic negotiations in which we are inevitably involved in ministry and in leadership of the church are human, mundane (sometimes painfully so). But Calvin's insight offers us a transcendent perspective on such dealings, which renders them significant beyond all human possibilities—because, as the poet Gerard Manley Hopkins wrote, "the world is charged with the grandeur of God."[23] At the same time, Calvin's insight relativizes the claims to our allegiance exerted by all of human knowledge—sociological, psychological, cultural, political, linguistic, and even theological—by showing us that such claims are subordinate to the full, ultimate, and sovereign claim of God.

What, then, would it mean for all forms of our ministry and service (whether as an ordained pastor, elder, deacon, or as a layperson) to be soaked in a baptism of awe and reverence? Surely it would mean, at least in part, that our lives would be saturated by an engagement with the holy, an encounter with God from which we can never fully recover. This engagement would shape our work of ministry and, indeed, our whole life. Therefore let us turn to consider what this transforming engagement with the holy looks like and explore how such engagement might reform our ministry and leadership.

Encountering the Transforming Presence of the Holy

God's holiness is referred to often in the Scriptures. Indeed, "the Holy One" (or "the Holy One of Israel") is an important way of naming God in the Bible. As my colleague Johanna van Wijk-Bos observes, in connection with God the word "holy" points to God's otherness, and was frequently the occasion for praise (as in Exod. 15:11; Pss. 77:13; 89:7; 99; 111:9; Isa. 6:3). Van Wijk-Bos writes,

> Typically, the contemplation of God's holiness causes both adoration and, at the same time, a consideration of human shortcomings in the face of God's splendid perfection. Isaiah therefore cries out that he is unclean and his people are unclean (6:5). The perception of human flaws causes fear or awe in the face of God's holiness.[24]

Further, the presence of the Holy One in the community's very midst issues a call: we are to be holy as God is holy (Lev. 19:2). That is, we are to act in holy (just, righteous) ways, just as God does—we are "to love the neighbor as the self (Lev. 19:18) and to love the stranger in the same way (19:34)."[25]

The many biblical accounts of human encounter with the Holy One—with this radically transcendent and radically immanent God who alone transforms us—include, for example, the story of God coming to Abram, first in a vision (Gen. 15:1–6), and then when a deep sleep had overcome Abram and "a deep and terrifying darkness" had descended upon him (Gen. 15:7–21). God speaks to Abram while he is in a liminal state—the state between what Abram had been and what he was called to become. God covenants with him in the deep and the darkness, in the realm of divine mystery, in the midst of smoke and fire. God transforms Abram the pilgrim into

Abraham the patriarch, and we see in the full cycle of Abraham stories the long pathway of transformation.

Another account (Gen. 32) tells of Jacob wrestling through the night with a divine messenger who resists all of Jacob's attempts at control and manipulation. The one with whom Jacob wrestled (a man, an angel, a god, God?) gave him a new name that signaled a new character: "You shall no longer be called Jacob [the sharp operator, the trickster, the con man], but Israel, for you have striven with God and with humans, and have prevailed" (Gen. 32:28). Jacob, convinced that the one with whom he wrestled was none other than God, went limping on his way throughout the remainder of his life, transformed but wounded.

From the story of Moses receiving the law on God's mountain, to the story of shattered Job's confrontation with God in the tempest; from the writings of awestruck psalmists, to those of prophets like Ezekiel and Isaiah—in the Bible we are confronted repeatedly by transforming encounters with "the living God."[26] Rudolf Otto, a religious scholar of another generation, argued in his classic study *The Idea of the Holy* that the phrase "the living God" differentiates the holy God of the Old Testament "from all mere 'world reason,' and becomes this ultimately non-rational essence, that eludes all philosophic treatment." Theologians and philosophers who later opposed the abstract and static deity of philosophy, favoring instead the "living God" of passion, love, and wrath, have "unwittingly been defending the non-rational core of the Biblical conception of God from all excessive rationalization."[27] Otto understood that the "rational and non-rational moment belong together in the idea of the Holy."[28] If we do not recognize this, then we emphasize one aspect at the expense of the other, falling into a wholly false irrationalism—or a wholly false rationalism.

At the height of the Enlightenment, philosopher J. G. Hamann raged against the soul-stultifying rationalism of his age: he argued that *God is not a mathematician but a poet,* and he rejected the "wide loathsome ditch" said by philosopher Gotthold Ephraim Lessing to separate human history from the eternal. Hamann was speaking in the name of the living God, the holy God of Abraham, Isaac, and Jacob, who had upturned his own life and his entire philosophical world in a crisis of spiritual transformation that forced him to reevaluate the nature of reality itself.[29] Hamann's experience was not unique. In fact, Hamann influenced Søren Kierkegaard, and through Kierkegaard he influenced generations of thinkers who have realized how narrow-minded reason can make us when we refuse to consider possibilities that do not easily fit our assumptions.

Rudolf Otto also helped us understand something that we Christians sometimes forget. The New Testament does not leave the living God—the Holy One—behind in the dust of a desert canyon on the Sinai Peninsula, or amid the shaken foundations of the prophet Isaiah's temple. John the Baptist rages in the grip of the holy. And it is in the name of this living God that the Baptist announces the coming of God's kingdom, in one whom he called "the Lamb of God" (John 1:36). The living God of Abraham, Isaac, and Jacob is the God and Father of our Lord Jesus Christ. Otto observes that as "heavenly Father" and "Lord" of the kingdom of heaven, God ". . . is not less, but far more 'holy,' 'numinous,' mysterious . . . *sacer*, and *sanctus* than His kingdom. He is all these in an absolute degree, and in this aspect of His nature He represents the sublimation and the consummation of all that the old covenant had grasped by way of 'creature-consciousness,' 'holy awe,' and the life."[30] Otto deliberately tries, I think, to disorient his reader. He stacks up unfamiliar descriptors of God and shifts from one language to another, from Hebrew to Greek to Latin—inviting the reader to sense the "otherness" of God, to feel that we are treading on holy ground in a region where bushes burst into flame with the Word of God, and where the stirring of every desert breeze might be a breath from God's mouth.

The sacred holiness expressed in the New Testament, Otto reminds us, is nowhere more characteristic than in the life of Jesus of Nazareth. Such holiness was particularly evident during that night in the Garden of Gethsemane, when the Son of Man prayed for God to let the cup pass. The agony of Jesus, the agony of a "soul shaken to its depths," expressed as sweat falling to the ground like drops of blood: this is no ordinary fear of death, according to Otto. "No, there is more here than the fear of death; there is the awe of the creature before the *mysterium tremendum*, before the shuddering secret of the numen."[31] Otto's reclaiming of unfamiliar phrases and his articulation of words half-remembered by conventional, slumbering piety propel his argument forward, reminding us that at the core of this faith that we share there is something beyond rationality, beyond (at least) *our* rational capacities.

Otto's conviction that encounter with the holy evokes shuddering or dread (*mysterium tremendum*) echoes Kierkegaard's discourse on the "fear and trembling" that are elicited when a person is brought to the reason beyond rationality, to the claim of holiness beyond aesthetics, and to the demand of the divine beyond morality into the realm of God alone.[32] The consequence of this encounter with the holy is a searing transformation: a passage through divine fire, through death. In Kierkegaard's case, this transformation threatened the superficial religious adherents to what he called "Christendom." Christendom is the kind of Christianity in which church members have been inoculated with just enough of the dead virus of religion that they are unlikely ever to catch the living faith of Christ. Kierkegaard's "fear and trembling" represents a life-changing experience with God, the kind of experience that Abraham had with a God who tested his faith by asking him to sacrifice his son, Isaac, only to withdraw the demand when it was clear that he would not even withhold his child from God. For Kierkegaard, it is essential to an experience of God that it cannot be classified among our other experiences, not even among our most moral experiences. If we do not draw back in revulsion and fear from such a God, Kierkegaard seems to say, it is not really God we have encountered.

Such a God challenges the logic of our theology, upending our assumptions about good and evil, right and wrong. While Kierkegaard's focus is on an individual's struggle of the soul, he assumes the presence of hearers of the biblical stories and readers of his recounting of the story. He assumes, in other words, that the individual encounter with God is at the heart of a genuine experience of the Christian community. Whereas some modern spirituality appears captive to a kind of solipsism of the soul, Kierkegaard urges us to confront the claim of God upon each of us, a claim that can draw us into a community of persons related to one another because of God's claim upon us all.

It is the transformative experience of God, at least in part, that the American psychologist of religion and philosopher William James tried to describe under the heading of "conversions," in his *Varieties of Religious Experience*.[33] Otto, Kierkegaard, and James each help us to remember that God will not be limited by our creeds or codes—indeed, that a genuine encounter with God plunges us into considerable cognitive dissonance, a disjunction between our conventional assumptions and God's claim upon us. God remains free to meet and to call whomever God wills on God's own terms. Nor is God's holiness to be construed as limiting God to a realm conveniently removed from this world. For the God of the Bible, holiness is a secular phenomenon and secularity is a province of the holy. God's holiness, as theologian Karl Barth (himself deeply influenced by Kierkegaard) has acknowledged, is not a feature of abstract transcendence, but of God's transcendent immanence. The closer God comes to us, the more deeply we are aware of God's radical otherness, the Godness of God.[34]

The dwelling of the Holy One among us, as wide as the whole of creation and as narrow as the smallest sanctuary, is the house of wonder, of awe, of reverence, of the holy. We should remember this above all else. Legend arose that long ago they tied a rope around the leg of the high priest of Israel so they could at least retrieve his body from the Holy of Holies should the presence of God overwhelm and kill him.

People yearn for an experience of the transcendent, we are told. People want an experience that can transform them, and give their lives meaning and significance. If pastors and leaders of the church are to address this yearning with faith and theological integrity, we must discover in our history and our own encounters with God how to teach our people to be attentive to the presence of the "sacred Other," the living God, who alone transforms us and gives our lives eternal significance. Our role is "priestly" in that we are building bridges of conscious awareness, so that our people take notice of that which has been there all along. We do so knowing that we cannot manipulate or control the results of any encounter with the living God. It is not our experiences (not even our religious experiences) that transform us spiritually, but God who does so. God is free to take us where God wills.

Emotions and affections are fleeting. Insights fade. Resolutions evaporate. If we try to manufacture experiences to transform the lives of the people who come to church, we will give them a counterfeit coin of our own minting in place of the genuine currency. And that is

an idolatrous business however we try to justify our actions. Changes
in persons based on even the liveliest emotional experiences cannot
be long sustained, but must be reinforced again and again by ever
more titillating experiences (more smoke! bigger mirrors!), the wor-
shiper descending into a spiral of vapid spiritual pornography. Only
the authentically holy transforms lives.

"It is a fearful thing to fall into the hands of the living God" (Heb.
10:31). But it is also a wondrous thing—death, but also resurrection—and it can come upon us in so many ways, whether unexpected
and unbeckoned, or long-desired at the close of a lifetime's quest.
Rudolf Otto spoke movingly of that experience of the holy which
may "come sweeping like a gentle tide, pervading the mind with a
tranquil mood of deepest worship." He continues:

> It may pass over into a more set and lasting attitude of the soul,
> continuing, as it were, thrillingly vibrant and resonant, until at
> last it dies away and the soul resumes its "profane," non-religious
> mood of everyday experience. It may burst in sudden eruption up
> from the depths of the soul with spasms and convulsions, or lead
> to the strangest excitements, to intoxicated frenzy, to transport,
> and to ecstasy. . . . [I]t may be developed into something beautiful
> and pure and glorious. It may become the hushed, trembling, and
> speechless humility of the creature in the presence of—whom or
> what? In the presence of that which is a *mystery* inexpressible and
> above all creatures.[35]

Whatever else we may say about this experience of becoming
aware of the presence of the holy, what must be clearly understood
is that it is the holy God who lays claim to us in the encounter. God
seeks not to produce merely a new experience in us, not even an
"intuition of absolute dependence," as important as such an intuition
is to our understanding ourselves in relationship to God. Rather, God
seeks to create a new humanity in the image of Jesus Christ, who
came to serve, not to be served.[36]

Jonathan Edwards described God in terms of the "*bonum formo-
sum*," the "beautiful good in itself." Edwards reminds us that the ultimate goal and highest good of Christian faith, ministry, and worship
is God, not something God does for us, and certainly just not some
benefit God gives us, but God alone.[37] Finding ourselves conscious

of the presence of the holy, the Sacred Other, the Being of being, the Life of life—here alone we know the measure of ourselves and what we are created and called to be. We know ourselves judged and graced, dead and risen. We know ourselves as dwelling in the house of God—a "house" which encompasses all of our Creator's work, which can never cease to be the house of wonder once we have encountered the holy there.

Docents in the House of Wonder

Abraham Heschel once spoke of "a life compatible with the presence of God," an existence conscious in each breath of the splendor and power and love of the Creator. "The awareness of the ineffable is that with which our search must begin," Heschel wrote.[38] If we were to engage in our ministries and leadership of the church as persons shaped by a radical perspective of divine encounter, what might this mean for the churches we lead? In ending, it is to this question I want to turn. In order to address it, I need to ask that we engage our imaginations to conjure a scene.

Imagine stepping into an ancient cathedral. The cathedral stands on tree-lined cliffs overlooking a deep and swiftly moving stream where centuries ago the hermit Saint Godric, of Frederick Buechner fame, bathed on the banks on which later Benedictine monks gathered their firewood and today families stroll with their dogs.[39] At either end of the cathedral lie the partial remains of other saints in places of prayer and quiet meditation: Saint Bede, called the Venerable, lies in quiet repose in a chapel clinging to a cliff above the river, while Saint Cuthbert is enshrined at the eastern end of the sanctuary behind the high altar.

Stepping into the cathedral you are blinded at first by the resolute shadows of the place. As the heavy oaken door closes behind you, and you enter the dark precincts, gingerly finding your way across the threshold, you are most aware that you have left the sun and sky and light of day beyond the door, and it takes a few moments to reorient yourself. Your eyes dilate. You become slowly accustomed to another, a very different, quality of light—light which, you realize, is streaming into the darkness in colored shafts through brilliantly

stained glass windows. It is as though you have entered into a jew-
eled box or been transported into a prism, through which simple
white light is transformed from merely spectral to something like a
performance of the sacred.

Making your way across the vast south aisle toward the nave
(even the strange vocabulary urges your dislocation from the world
outside) you are struck both by the antiquity and immense scale of
the cathedral. Columns a thousand years old stretch toward a ceiling
more than a hundred feet above you. You feel small and insignifi-
cant, like a mote of space debris drifting into the gravitational pull
of a supernova, as you walk along the central aisle toward the sound
of a choir softly intoning the Psalter. Echoes return the length of the
nave like a remembrance of the hint of an aroma of incense on the
stirrings of a draft of air.

Making your way up the long central aisle toward the choir, a man
robed in scarlet appears from the shadows and approaches you. He
is a docent—an appointed guide—in this cathedral. He loves this
place, and it is his vocation to share the sanctuary with others who
visit. He offers to walk with you. You have been here before. You
have walked these aisles. You have looked upon these tombs, and
carvings, and windows. You do not feel particularly in need of a
guide, but you welcome the fellowship, so you accept his invitation
to join him.

As you walk together, the docent points out first this stone, then
this seat in the choir. There, he points, sits the Bishop of Durham
when the dean invites him to preside, though the bishop cannot preside without the dean's invitation, whether or not he is a bishop or
a prince besides. There is the tomb of one of the greatest lords of
Northumbria, though not one of the most pious. The docent points
out the change in colors of building stone that indicates where the
Norman Romanesque cathedral ends and the later Gothic addition
begins, each crease in the wall telling us that once a private chapel
stood here, and there.

He points out the damage the "Presbyterians" did when Cromwell
billeted his troops and stabled their horses in the cathedral. He points
out the marks that axes and swords made on the tombs as the soldiers
hacked off heads and defaced the effigies of long-departed knights
and ladies and bishops. He shows you the book of remembrance for

coal miners, the names of every miner in the region who died in a cave-in or an explosion carefully inscribed. A page is turned each day. There are many pages.

As he quietly points here and tells a story there, you become aware of layer upon layer of life and death, of praises and laments, held secret in the cathedral's walls. These are secrets you did not know. You become aware also that the docent is telling you more than stories.

The docent is also telling you he has met the holy in this place. He is hinting that you can too.

You remember your previous visit to this cathedral, guidebook in hand, a mere liturgical tourist in the midst of a majestic ecclesiastical edifice. For all the beauty you saw then, it was a flat visit by comparison, at best an exercise in historical curiosity and, perhaps, romanticism. Today, the docent has escorted you to the verge of something wholly different. With the docent at your side, you have been helped across another threshold. Your eyes, with his help, have become accustomed to seeing in the dark. Today the docent has helped you to be transformed from a tourist into a pilgrim.

Together you make your way to a place behind and below the high altar, a low tomb of plain, dark marble. In the candlelight you see the name of the saint carved deeply in its surface. You sense that you have reached the climax of this intimate tour. You sense also that you have been steered here on purpose by the docent's cunning and skill. The docent tells you in whispers what it means to him as a person of faith that Christians worship here, and have worshiped here for fourteen hundred years. He speaks of the saint whose bones lie at your feet as though he were speaking of a father or a mother he loves and with whom he still speaks each day. He tells you of wonders others have experienced praying on these very stones. He tells you he prays here. His words, simple and humble, touch you. And as the docent slips away to greet another tourist, you find yourself bowing also to pray.

Rudolf Otto says of the consciousness of "the holy" that it cannot be "taught," only "awakened."[40] It is this task of wakening that we need to reclaim and place at the heart of ministry and church leadership, at the heart of congregational life.

Hidden within every practice of faith, every act of ministry, and each gathering of the community of faith, there is the possibility of encounter with the Sacred Other, the Holy One who alone transforms humanity. The docent is in the midst of it all, communicating, shepherding, and leading. The docent points here and there, sets velvet ropes around the mysteries in our midst, and encourages us to notice what a dozen times before we walked past without noticing.

When a docent is unskilled and ignorant, lacking in experience of divine things and the wisdom that such experience brings, we are unlikely to notice much of the sacred among us. Indeed, in these cases the sacred can actually be obscured by the docent. A poor docent is more likely to attract attention to him- or herself than to the holy.

Congregational leadership and church administration, in such cases, can remain bone-dry, soul-stultifying, an annoyance both to the leaders and to those who are led. With the unskilled docent we are not likely to perceive leadership as an equipping of God's saints for the sake of God's mission, but only as paperwork, endless lists of jobs to be done, and committee positions to be filled. Sometimes the inadequate docent may even give the impression that the ministries of "a people of God" hardly matter at all, but that only his or her own ministry matters. The unskilled docent points not to God in Christ but to him- or herself.

Preaching, in the hands of an unskilled docent, falls into the dull repetition of truisms and prepackaged clichés or into the vain business of pastoral self-promotion. Shepherding becomes merely people-pleasing with no concept that it is to the pleasure of God we all are called. However pleased people may be with us, they will not in the end thank us if we give them a mess of pottage, as Karl Barth once said, when they are coming to church longing passionately "to lay hold of [the God] who overcomes the world because he is its Creator and Redeemer, its beginning and end and Lord."[41] They come, as Barth once observed, longing to know the answer to one question, "Is it true?" They come, their own lives embodying that question, longing to encounter the Truth that is none other than the holy God who shatters our untruth with a love that will not let us go until we are transformed.

Richard Lischer goes a long way toward describing the vocation of the competent docent in his profound memoir of ministry in a Midwestern Lutheran congregation. Lischer writes,

Our journey in Cana [his congregation] was Pilgrim's journey, if not to the Heavenly City, at least toward the fullest expression of the life that had been given us. "The glory of God is humanity fully alive," St. Irenaeus said. If he was right, I saw the glory of God many times where I least expected it. . . . The only thing that made us different from any other kinship group or society was the mysterious presence of Jesus in the community. We were his body, which is not a metaphor. The ordinary world really *is* capable of hosting the infinite Being. As I searched the face of my congregation on my last Sunday, I felt the theological point was proved.[42]

The vocation of the docent is to discern and to assist us in discerning God at work among us. This vocation by necessity is lived out in the most pedestrian ways imaginable. But pedestrian as its ways may be, this vocation is a living invitation to discover the mystery of the Lord's Table at every turn. The docent invites us: "Lift up your hearts." And, as we discern the presence of God gathering around the sacrament of Holy Communion, or breaking bread with family and friends, or serving soup to the homeless, or sharing a cup of coffee with someone from whom we have been long estranged, "our hearts are lifted up into the presence of God." This vocation invites us to live the mystery of baptism. The docent wades out into a mighty rushing stream that, unseen by many, floods the streets of our cities and towns. With an outstretched hand, she invites us to remember that all of us who have been baptized into Christ Jesus have been baptized into his death, drowned in these waters. Our sin was nailed to Christ's cross. We were buried with him so that "as Christ was raised from the dead by the glory of the Father, so we too might walk in newness of life" (Rom. 6:4). The mundane activities and the ordinary relationships that define our days constitute the playhouse in which God's glory is performed.

Many people, we are told—and I believe it is true—are coming to church today longing for a transforming experience with the transcendent God. How disappointed some must be to find there just more of the same vain entertainment and marketing, nationalistic jingoism, self-promotion, and party-interest that they hoped they had left outside. But it need not be so, and a recovery of our vocation as docents in the house of wonder could, I believe, go a long way toward responding to what people want in a way that people need.

Our docents in the church are all who share a calling to serve as ushers at the threshold of the holy. Those who answer this call are both ordained and unordained, and in the best circumstances make up a mighty company in a congregation. Their vocation is to deliver people into an awareness of the presence of God, in which they will know themselves to be creatures created for God's own gracious, good, and just ends. It is a vocation that is at once sacred, irreducible, and foolish by all worldly standards (see 1 Cor. 1:27–29). Docents point out to us the signs of God's presence among us, walk with us to that place where the holy is to be found, and teach us to live with reverence and serve with awe in the house of the Lord—a house that includes our houses of worship but also extends into all the world.

Docents' task—showing people into the very presence of God—is, of course, an impossible one. But competent docents in the house of wonder help to set the conditions for the impossible to occur again and again: telling a story here, reminding us by a gesture there, now whispering, now remaining silent, marking a boundary with care, then admitting us beyond the velvet ropes into the Holy of Holies. In setting these conditions, docents deny their own efficacy, protesting that God cannot be made known by human efforts. God is free. God is sovereign, unfettered, and unbounded. The free and living God wills to transform us into the likeness of Jesus Christ using all sorts and conditions of instruments, even the instrumentality of humble docents.

Chapter 6

Theological Education
and the Reformed Project

The Reformed project has always promoted theological education to
support and strengthen the church in its mission. We live at a moment,
however—an axial moment in the history of the church—when some
question the rationale for the theological education of those called to
lead the church. Today we must argue convincingly for a theologically well-educated ministry if we care about the quality of preaching
and the worship of God, of pastoral care and counseling, of Christian teaching and nurture, of mission, service, and evangelism. We
must make this argument powerfully if we care about the nurturing
of a church that can grapple with the social and cultural challenges it
faces. Theological education will not solve every problem: it will not
heal our every disease or deliver us from every evil. But theological
education can teach us that we don't have to be mean or stupid to
follow Jesus of Nazareth. And in our culture today, this is one of the
most countercultural messages we can articulate.

The Moment

Over the past few years, I have become increasingly familiar with
MapQuest and the various GPS devices that help us navigate our
roadways. I can't remember now what we did without them, though
I do have a vague recollection of being lost fairly often. I also have
some memory of certain intense conversations occurring in our car
in which my spouse said, "Why don't you just stop and ask directions?" And I responded, "I'm sure that the last street we passed

was where we should have turned." Technology, mercifully, has made those conversations less frequent. But, I've discovered that I still find it helpful to buy maps for one simple reason: I want to know where I am in relation to where I am bound. I want a complete orientation to my journey so that I can imagine the whole thing. In other words, I want to know more than just what my next turn should be.

Sometimes—and this is true of both travel and life in general—we locate ourselves *temporally* as much as *spatially*. Sometimes knowing *where* we are means knowing *when* we are.

Pondering the church's "location" today, I have become convinced that we are living in an exceptional historical moment, at least for Protestant Christianity: a moment I would characterize as *axial*.

The term "axial" was first applied as a historical metaphor by Karl Jaspers, a prolific and influential philosopher of the twentieth century. Jaspers tried to account for the rise of humanity's self-consciousness and the emergence of many of the great spiritual traditions by pointing to *an axis of world history* around which our intellectual, moral, and spiritual history turns. He identified a specific historical era (between 800 and 200 BCE) when Confucius and Lao-Tzu lived in China, the Buddha came to prominence in India, Zarathustrian thought first emerged in ancient Persia, Heraclitus and Plato taught in Greece, and Hebrew prophets burst upon the scene in Palestine. This was a time of terror, Jaspers observed, an age of radical questioning, when settled orthodoxies were subjected to fresh examination and the basic ends of human existence were renegotiated.[1]

The intellectual and spiritual history of humanity, according to Jaspers, turned around this axial age, this axis of history, and as it turned the entire human world was unsettled by the turning. The trajectories that arced from this axial age into the present were divergent in convictions and doctrines. The spiritual paths of renunciation and of embrace; of solitude, meditation and prayer; of social justice and wisdom; of prophecy as an ecstatic experience and as a proclamation of God's reign can all be traced to the refracted light that illuminated humankind in those centuries. Humanity, Jaspers tells us, "took a forward leap" in this time, but it was a leap predicated on struggle, uncertainty, and ambiguity.[2]

Today we also live in an axial age. Ours may not be the same in scale or in effect as that which Jaspers described. But, I have found Jasper's metaphor helpful in understanding the moment in which we live, especially as Protestant Christians. Whether we are in conversation with James Davison Hunter's fascinating recent study, *To Change the World,* in which he reflects on what he describes as "the irony, the tragedy and possibility of Christianity in the late modern world"; or with Kathryn Tanner's brilliant theological analysis of contemporary postmodern culture; or with economist Robert William Fogel's sweeping study of a trans-cultural "fourth Great Awakening"; or with any number of other recent sociological, political, economic, or theological theories accounting for the various movements of the tectonic plates on which our cultural continents ride, this much is clear: we have become peculiarly conscious of our precarious position in the world, and many of the certainties of our childhood have been shaken.[3] Modernity, post-modernity, and a score or so of other post-adjectival-modifiers locate us in a time in which so much is up for grabs that we are having a hard time discerning who we are, where we are, what we should do, and where we should go.

Theological schools are right in the middle of this axial moment, because the church is right in the middle of this moment.[4] Most if not all of the issues that challenge the church also challenge the seminaries. And among the issues that challenge us most today is the one issue that called seminaries into existence in the first place: *the theological education of persons for ordained ministry.*

In certain ecclesiastical circles it has become commonplace today to say that seminary education is unnecessary for those who will lead our congregations and provide leadership for various forms of ministry in society.

Well, I would like to confirm to you that seminary education is indeed *unnecessary.* The critics of graduate-level theological education are correct on this point. It is unnecessary to be biblically and theologically educated in order to carry out many of the basic ministerial functions. Rudimentary training is sufficient for most folks to get the right end of the baby wet, or to pour juice and serve crackers while saying the prescribed words. And it takes virtually no training at all, except basic computer skills, to steal a good sermon—though one might argue that it takes considerable theological knowledge to figure out which sermon you ought to steal.

The point that I want to make is that we are asking the wrong question when we inquire whether it is necessary to have a seminary education in order to perform acts of ministry.

The right question, and the question that brought seminaries and other forms of theological education into existence in the first place—the question that has endured not for a hundred years nor even for five hundred years, but that has been around for two thousand years—is more complicated. Indeed, it is a twofold question: *What quality of ministry best serves the gospel?* and *How do we best prepare persons for that quality of ministry?* The question, in other words, is not one of *minimal qualifications to fulfill ecclesiastical functions.* It concerns, rather, the types, qualities, and character of leadership our church needs if it is to thrive, to flourish, to "be filled with all the fullness of God" (Eph. 3:19). What kind of ministers can cultivate a reflective and transformative faith among the people of God, helping them to envision and to live the sort of "life that truly is life-giving in and for the sake of the world?"[5]

There have been few moments in Christianity's history when more was at stake than at this moment. There have been few moments in Christianity's history when we have needed a thinking faith, a theologically reflective faith, a generous and critical, imaginative and deeply engaged faith more than we do today.

We live at a moment—an axial moment for Protestant Christianity—when the arguments for an educated ministry can no longer be taken for granted. We must argue persuasively today for an educated ministry if we care about the *quality* of preaching and worship of God, the *quality* of pastoral care and counseling, the *quality* of Christian teaching and nurture, the *quality* of mission and service and evangelism.

I do not know if my arguments will prove convincing. But I hope that my comments, if they do nothing else, will encourage each of us to come up with our own cases for a well-informed, knowledgeable, wise, and well-educated ministry, because I want to share a little nonsecret with you: *We're losing this argument in today's culture.* And I think we're losing this argument primarily because we have taken the importance of an educated ministry for granted for so long.

There are forces in our culture that thrive on reductionism, super-stition, and hatred—forces that work overtime to promote ignorance in the name of piety and the advancement of fear and anxiety in the name of devotion. There are forces in our culture that despise critical thinking, especially when it comes to religious faith. These forces appreciate the value of propaganda and the kind of religious training and indoctrination that marches in step. But they look upon genuine theological education as a threat to faith.

The cost could hardly be higher. Many of us were reminded in the summer of 2010 of the costs of an uneducated church when a sincere and zealous minister of a congregation in Florida grabbed the public microphone for a good deal longer than his allotted fifteen minutes of fame and called upon fellow Christians around the world to burn the holy book of another faith (one he admitted to having read only in part[6]) to show their devotion to Jesus. We were further reminded early in 2011 when the same minister, now operating largely without a congregation but with the benefit of an even wider audience followed through on his threat by holding a mock trial and execution of the Qur'an.

The cost could hardly be higher. We have read the awful stories of a congregation from Topeka, Kansas, whose members, because of their religiously inspired hatred of people who do not share their moral values, protest the funerals of fallen American military. The fact that they have a constitutionally guaranteed right to express their opinions does not mean that their message is any less hateful.

The cost could hardly be higher to our society and to the world if we opt for an uneducated church.

We do not ask for the moment history gives us. History is thrust upon us all. But make no mistake about it: this is our moment, our axial age, when the world turns upon its temporal axis. We must either stand up to be counted for a thinking faith or stand idly by on the sidelines while hatred, prejudice, intolerance, and every form of violence take their turns doing their worst in the name of God.

Education alone will not solve every problem, not even theologi-cal education. We know this. Education alone will not heal our every disease or deliver us from every evil. But theological education can teach us that we don't have to be mean or stupid to follow Jesus of Nazareth. And in our culture today, this is one of the most counter-cultural messages we can articulate.

The church always stands just one generation, just one short step away from the sort of narrow-mindedness and reactivity against others that we've seen on our television screens a hundred times or that we have felt rising up in ourselves in our own worst moments, when the better angels of our souls struggled against our own inner demons, when we felt threatened, worried, or anxious. Therefore I want to argue for education—for graduate-level theological education of a particular quality and kind—for the sake of the church's life and ministry in God's world.

There are several contributions to the life and faith of the church that theological education makes and that nothing else can do quite as well. Theological education *informs*, certainly, transmitting important facts from one generation to another. It also *forms* persons in faith and for ministry, allowing them to mature into the kinds of people suited to lead congregations. But among the things theological education does best, and the reason it is so important, is because it also *transforms* persons. Theological education transforms persons specifically for public ministry. It is able to do this because the content and the subject matter of theological education is the gospel of Jesus Christ, which *transforms* us and invites us into *the ministry of transformation*. Theological education changes us in fundamental ways.

This has been, of course, the deep suspicion of generations of worried folks who have sent their students off to seminary with the warning that it will destroy their faith. I am here to tell you that (in some sense) their fears are warranted.

When theological education works, it does (again, *in some sense*) destroy our faith. At least, it challenges and calls into question, it critiques and examines and sometimes dismantles the *faith we brought to seminary*. It does this because such reshaping of faith from the ground up is essential for the making of ministers who can lead the church in its ministry of grace and justice for the sake of God's world.

A year or two years or ten years after graduation from seminary, a former student (by then a minister) stands at the door of the emergency room as the ambulance pulls up, and the small body of a child run over while participating in her church's CROP Walk is pulled out on the gurney—and that minister is the person who holds the family in her arms and in her prayers as their world collapses around them. It is at this moment when the minister knows that if her faith had not been dismantled brick by brick and rebuilt with critical attention to details she never imagined before seminary, and if the Walls of Jericho had not fallen around her head in her class on the Hebrew Scriptures, then she would have no firm foundation today when that family needs her to be a source of strength, wisdom, and comfort for them.

A year or two years or ten years after graduation from seminary, a former student (by then in leadership of a congregation)—a former student who, at the beginning of seminary, protected with reinforced walls the faith he brought to seminary, defending it against every onslaught of critical argument—that student will preach after planes fly into tall buildings and the wreckage scatters across the heart of a nation. And, standing amid the wreckage, when many are calling for hatred and vengeance, and something else even more difficult to name that would sacrifice the message of Christ's cross in a heartbeat to buy a measure of national security, then this minister knows that the faith he brought to seminary had to die if he is ever to preach what the author of the Letter to the Hebrews calls "a better resurrection."

Theological education transforms us so we can lead the church as the church engages in its ministry of grace and justice for the sake of God's world.

Certainly, theological education *informs* us. But it's not the information alone that we need. Certainly, theological education also *forms* us. But, as important as formation is, it falls short. Theological education necessarily *transforms* us, because only if we have passed through the crucible of transformation can we believe strongly enough so that we can doubt what has always been accepted or imagine what has never before been seen.

The transformative power of theological education is not restricted to graduate-level seminary education. Every one of us has known the power of theological education to transform, through sermons, Bible studies, mission trips, and counseling sessions. God meets us through all of these means of grace, and again and again we are reminded that "our God is a consuming fire" (Heb. 12:29) who purges, changes, and refines us through the flames of divine love—often by presenting us with utterly new ways to understand ourselves in relation to God and others.

At its heart, Christianity is a learned faith—and a faith that always calls us to learn more. We are all transformed through the

renewing of our minds (Rom. 12:1–2), as Paul said, and the ministry of transformation to which God calls us is for all God's people.
But, in order for this ministry of transformation to flourish, we need
those who lead our congregations to lead from the crucible of their
own deep transformation. This transformation begins for all of us
in our encounter with the message of what the late A. B. Rhodes
once described as "the mighty acts of God."[7]

The Message

In one of the most remarkable books on congregational ministry in
recent years, Lillian Daniel and Martin Copenhaver's *This Odd and
Wondrous Calling,* the authors explore the theological dimensions
of ordinary acts of ministry. In my favorite chapter, in which Copenhaver reflects on shaking hands at the door of the church after worship, he provides the conclusion to the last sermon he preached in
one of his congregations. The sermon was titled simply, "What It's
All About." He preached,

> As I am about to leave, there is something I want to tell you. I want
> to tell you what Jesus means to me. I want to share my belief that
> everything depends on him. I want to urge you to learn from him.
> I want to assure you that you can lean on him in times of trouble.
> I want to ask you to listen to his words of challenge. I want to tell
> you that I believe that you can entrust your life to him. I want to
> affirm that he is Lord of this church, and that in his name you are
> freed to love one another and empowered to share that love with
> a hurting world. I want to profess that, though once people could
> not look at the face of God and live, now we are invited to look at
> the face of God in him, in Jesus, and live as we have never lived
> before. He is Emmanuel, God with us, God with us all, whether
> we are together or apart. That's what it's all about. That's all I
> know. Amen.[8]

There are so many ways to articulate this central message of our
faith—so many places that we may encounter it.
    As a teenager, my world was turned upside down, and I was set on
a path that led to my call to the ministry of Word and Sacrament by
reading Leo Tolstoy's writings on Christianity. I did not know then

about the ways in which Tolstoy's message had influenced Mohandas Gandhi, or Dietrich Bonhoeffer, or Martin Luther King Jr. Years later, when I had become a pastor, I heard this message translated into the cadences of a distinctly Southern idiom by Clarence Jordan of the Koinonia Farm in Georgia: Jordan reached out to me with convicting power through his Cotton Patch Gospel, reminding me that "faith is not belief in spite of evidence, but a life in scorn of the consequences."[9]

Sometimes the message emphasizes God's reign, as in James Luther Mays's marvelous writings on the Psalms; or God's humanity, as in the writings of the late Karl Barth; or God's justice, as in the works of Abraham Joshua Heschel. Sometimes the message can touch us with the irony and tragic comedy of the human condition and the intractability of the call of God, as in the short stories of Flannery O'Connor and Miguel de Unamuno or the novels of Marilynne Robinson. There are times in which the one thing we must hear in the message is the awesome vastness of the God who is *within* yet *beyond* all existence—whether that vastness is expressed ecstatically by Jonathan Edwards, or with the awesome precision of process theology, or with the beautiful and searing doubt of Louise Glück's poetry.

Or the message can, with José Míguez-Bonino, challenge us to be less concerned about theoretical matters like the question of God's existence and much more exacting in our allegiance to the God who liberates: "In truth," Míguez-Bonino writes, "the important thing is precisely in *which* God we believe. . . . It is . . . significant that the early Christians were accused of being atheists and were judged and condemned as such for refusing to believe in the ruling gods of their society."[10]

The various components or mechanisms of the educational process, such as the lectures, the papers, the seminars, and so forth, are crucial elements in the wondrous alchemy of theological education, but by themselves they do not transform us. The *subject matter* and *content* of theological education—the message and, indeed, the very presence of the Holy One to whom we bear witness—are what transform us. It is *the God to whom we bear witness through the gospel* who transforms us—the God who, though we were far off, met us in Jesus Christ and brought us home.

Our emphases in articulating this message will differ according to time and culture and historical context, but it is still the message of our most ancient mothers and fathers in the faith: "Hear, O Israel: the

LORD is our God, the LORD alone. You shall love the LORD your God with all your heart, and with all your soul, and with all your might" (Deut. 6:4–5).

The message is still the message of the Prophets, from the God who cares more about justice that rolls down like a mighty rushing stream than about religious observances (Amos 5:18–24), the God who requires above all that we love mercy, do justice, and walk humbly with our God (Micah 6:6–8).

The message is still that of the Christ of John's Gospel: "I came that they may have life, and have it abundantly" (John 10:10b). It is still the message of the Jesus of Mark's Gospel: "If any want to become my followers, let them deny themselves and take up their cross and follow me. For those who want to save their life will lose it, and those who lose their life for my sake, and for the sake of the gospel, will save it" (Mark 8:34–35).

The message is still that of Peter addressing the crowds at Pentecost: "Jesus of Nazareth, a man attested to you by God with deeds of power, wonders, and signs that God did through him among you, as you yourselves know—this man, handed over to you according to the definite plan and foreknowledge of God, you crucified and killed by the hands of those outside the law. But God raised him up, having freed him from death, because it was impossible for him to be held in its power" (Acts 2:22–24).

The message is still that which transformed Saul into Paul: "As many of you as were baptized into Christ have clothed yourselves with Christ. There is no longer Jew or Greek, there is no longer slave or free, there is no longer male and female; for all of you are one in Christ Jesus" (Gal. 3:27–28).

The message never grows tiresome. The message always surprises. And the study of the meanings of this message is the core work of theological education.

The Meaning

Spoken in a thousand varied accents the world over, throughout the centuries, the message is at its heart and soul that of the God who became like us in Jesus of Nazareth so that we could be restored to our full humanity in Christ. Theological education conveys this message from one generation to another, but with a critical edge. At times theological education critiques the powers and principalities that would attempt to make this message simply another commodity to be traded or another version of its own most precious story of self-actualization (that is, salvation by works). At other times theological education critiques even ministry itself, when, for example, ministry imitates the sins of Simon Magus, who desired the gospel as a tool to his own ends of self-promotion and power. At still other times theological education conveys the core message while also criticizing our human tendency to make God over in our own image. And sometimes, theological education conveys this message with a remarkable intimacy, inviting us (in the words of one popular scholar) to "meet Jesus again for the first time."[11]

When theological education performs its task best, it challenges us to get ourselves out of the way for the sake of our own redemption. It reminds us that we are not infinitely adorable, but that God is. The promise of the gospel is not that wherever we are lifted up, all people will be drawn to us, but that wherever Christ is lifted up, there humanity will find salvation.

Theological education also reminds us that however morally compromised even our highest standards may be, God is faithful and just, and works through imperfect people and processes to realize God's own ends. We recognize as Christians that the Holy Spirit works through the tangles of human history, through the manipulations of church courts, commissions, and councils, and even through the vagaries of political decision making in civil and uncivil society to accomplish God's purposes in history. So also we must recognize that the Holy Spirit is at work in and through the critical research of scholars from John Calvin to Rebecca Chopp, clearing away the undergrowth of superstition, romanticism, and idealism that can choke out a bracing, true encounter with the gospel that changes lives and worlds.

There are varieties of theological work, Rowan Williams once observed, including the celebrative theology that we enact and speak, sing and represent through visual arts and dance; the communicative theology that attempts to bridge the boundaries separating theology and science, medicine, psychology, philosophy, cultural studies, and the arts; and the critical theology that examines with meticulous care the texts we hold sacred and the content of our doctrine. While theological education participates in every kind of theological work, from celebration to critical study, its primary task lies arguably in the last of these: critical engagement with texts and doctrine.[12]

This focus is necessary not only because the scholar's work, at least since the Renaissance and certainly since the Enlightenment, has been informed by a range of historical methods and philosophical assumptions that must be intelligently engaged (although they do not determine the meaning of the gospel in every encounter with it). No, quite apart from the methods and assumptions that have emerged in scholarship during the past five hundred years, the scholar's task has *always* required faithful analytical work. It is not only for their piety that we still value Gregory of Nyssa or Friedrich Schleiermacher. We value the sharpness of their critical theological reflections. They help us think more clearly about what we believe.

Theological studies have served the church best when theology has asked its critical questions freely. Origen's creative and critical articulation of the implications of the gospel message led both to the heresy of Arius and the orthodoxy of Athanasius. We must recognize that the relationship between church and scholarship has been stressed especially on the point of the essential critical work of theological studies. John McLeod Campbell and William Robertson Smith's scholarship, which today appears utterly within the bounds of churchly endeavors (even within the bounds of evangelical devotion), was judged heretical not that long ago.

The critical task of theological education, which can, in its more strident forms, irritate the church, remains one of the church's greatest gifts to itself, stretching us at exactly those points where we can grow most complacent, and asking our next generation of leaders and ministers to reflect in ways that open up new and unexpected paths of faithfulness. It may be that it is precisely at this point that theological schools make their greatest contribution to society as well.

A few years ago, an article by W. Robert Connor appeared in the *Chronicle of Higher Education* on a problem faced in many college and university classrooms. Students, it was reported, are bringing to their college classrooms questions many of their college professors feel hesitant or ill-equipped to answer. Students are bringing into university classrooms questions of ultimate meaning and purpose, asking "Why am I here?" and "Does my life have meaning?"[13] And virtually any pastor knows that the biggest question still asked in virtually every congregation is the question of evil and suffering: "How can a good God allow such suffering in this world?" While professors in many college classrooms may wish to avoid such questions (and, of course, it depends on which universities and which class rooms), it is the bread and butter of theological education to wrestle with all of these questions. The seminary is the Big Question destination, where any and every subject can be placed on the table, poked, prodded, examined, and turned over and over again.

Thomas Merton once described the spiritual discipline of contemplation in these words: "It is as if in creating us God asked a question, and in awakening us to contemplation [God] answered the question, so that the contemplation is at the same time, question and answer."[14] The critical task of theological education—the task of grappling with the meanings in the message of the gospel and the meanings of our humanity in light of the God of the gospel—is both a critical and a contemplative task, embodying both the question and the answer, allowing our human existence to be subjected to the critical, interrogatory examination of the message, and allowing ourselves, through the freedom given us in the gospel of Jesus Christ, to interrogate the message in light of our lives.

It is in and through this extraordinary and critical theological engagement of our humanity and the message of the gospel that we are transformed. And it is this engagement that happens every day in seminary. This is the magic of theological education.

The Magic

There is something magical in the chemistry of the classroom when a gifted teacher in the grip of her subject, in love with her subject, in possession of her subject, even possessed by her subject, comes into contact with learners who are ready—even when the readiness presents itself as a resistance to the subject. In these moments, the task of inquiring into the meanings of the message is transformed. Magic ensues.

This is why great lectures are still great. But there is a genius in theological education beyond even this kind of genius. There is also, and even more importantly, the genius of the communal learning experience, when students and teachers who know one another well and live among one another learn together.

There are so many examples of how this occurs in graduate theological education, but at the seminary I serve, Louisville Presbyterian Theological Seminary, one course, in particular, assumed almost legendary status, a seminar that was co-taught by Craig Dykstra and Burton Cooper in the fall of 1982 through January of 1983.

We are told in the description of the course in its syllabus that this "experimental course" is "designed to overcome the dichotomy between classroom learning and ministerial practice. The theme of the course is the Christian understanding of God as that understanding relates to the presence of evil and suffering in human life and to our ability to endure such evil and suffering without falling into bitterness or resignation." But the syllabus only hints at what actually happened in this course.

The students had to apply to become members of the seminar. They had to agree to take on an exceptionally heavy workload, not just reading in theology and philosophy and literature, viewing films and so forth, but also writing sermons, reflecting on case studies from their own ministry contexts and crafting statements of faith in light of what they were learning.

The course won a Grawemeyer Award for excellence in teaching.[15] But, the real prize was the transformation of the students *and* the professors, as they will tell you to this very day.

Recently I asked one of the students from this class what it meant to him. This student, incidentally, is now one of our professors at Louisville Seminary, Bradley Wigger. He says that what he learned in that course thirty years ago has stayed with him to this day. Brad said, "I can't think about evil and suffering without thinking about the case studies, the sermons, the situations the students brought to class. Their voices are still present in me: the professors, students, and others who suffered."

Burton Cooper's subsequent book, *Why, God?* owed a great deal to this course, as he brought his own personal experience of suffering into the critical study and invited a group of students to learn with him.[16] When I asked Craig Dykstra about this course, the word he used to characterize its effect on him was "transformative."

Most of us who have been through theological education could relate our own stories of transformation. We could all bear witness to moments in an experience of clinical pastoral education or theological field education when a wise supervisor deftly guided us to see something that we had studiously avoided, but which, if it had been left untouched, might have festered into soul sickness—a condition that could have infected and undermined our ministry in years to come. We could tell of moments of critical analysis in a therapeutic practicum or in spiritual direction, when secrets we kept (even from ourselves) were revealed, and we were healed through confession and an assurance of pardon from unexpected sources. We could recall lectures, seminars, or study groups when Greek verbs, or ecumenical councils, or historical-critical studies of ancient texts yielded more than information, when we found ourselves standing in the presence of the God of the ages, forgiven and judged and called to serve.

The magic of theological education does not turn base metals into gold. It does something much more crucial. Through the wonder of theological education we are ushered into a deeper encounter with the world around us, a world that God creates and holds in existence. We are taught to acquire a humility and awe, a reverence toward God and respect for others that are irreplaceable and essential attributes of effective ministry.

In the journey of theological education, seminaries are not terminals, they are launching pads. That is why the final event of our degree program is called commencement. The adventure of theological education is intended to prepare us to serve intelligently and faithfully. To be theologically well-educated is not to become bookish, but to become wise.

What happens in theological schools has the potential to change the world for all time. Amid silence, voices, and sighs; in the glow of computer monitors in the library and candles in the sanctuary; in ministry settings in the midst of the city, or down a country lane; over meals in the cafeteria, around tables in our homes—in short, wherever "classrooms" happen, here we touch the core of life, here we touch God, and here, together, we are transformed through the renewing of our minds.

Theological education is as unnecessary as ministry. Nothing hangs on it—except the quality of our faith and our life together as a people of God.

Chapter 7

A Forgotten Hallmark
of the Reformed Project

The biblical, theological, and churchly legacy we have inherited as Reformed Christians is an extraordinary gift. Among the most remarkable and vital hallmarks of our Reformed legacy there is one that is often forgotten: Innovation, the capacity to draw from the experience of ancient Christian communities and to adapt these lessons to new situations. This Reformed innovation underlies its whole history. From its beginnings, the Reformed project has demonstrated a capacity to adapt and change to new conditions in new environments and to do so in ways that remain appropriate to who we are called to be as a community of followers of Jesus Christ. What's next for the Reformed project is to recover the sense of adventure—to fire our theological imaginations again and to find the courage we need to participate with the Christ who is already "doing a new thing" in the world around us.

But We've Always Done It This Way

Several years ago I was in a lively conversation with a colleague about a proposal then before the church to ordain Christian educators. His position was that because the Presbyterian Church historically had only authorized three ordained offices—deacons, elders, and ministers of the Word and Sacrament (or, deacons, ruling elders, and teaching elders)—we simply had no authority to devise other offices.

"That's true—but only in part," I responded.

My reasoning went as follows.

Historically speaking, Presbyterians did settle on the three ordained positions he mentioned. But we're missing something really important in our story as Presbyterians if that's all we see here. We're missing the variety of offices and roles described in the New Testament from which we might have chosen and might still choose, should the Spirit of God lead the church to do so: bishops, teachers, prophets, and evangelists, among them (see Acts 7; Rom. 16; 1 Cor. 12; 2 Cor. 11; 1 Tim. 3; 1 Pet. 5; 2 Pet. 2 for the origins and characteristics of, exhortations for, and warnings about various offices and roles in the early church).

We're missing something else too. We're missing what we might call the forgotten hallmark of Presbyterianism: *Innovation.*

The Reformed project, at its best, has been characterized by innovation—a capacity to draw from the deep experiences of the early Christian communities and to adapt the lessons of those experiences to new environments and emerging situations. This is something the Reformed movement received as a resource from the early church.

John Calvin and other great reformers looked at the sacraments that had evolved in the medieval Roman Catholic Church, and they exercised a particular form of innovation. First, they weighed the church's practices with regard to the sacraments against the biblical witness, having committed always to reform the church within the authority of the Bible. Second, they weighed the church's practices against those of early Christianity, especially through the apostolic and patristic ages. Third, they weighed the church's practices against the needs of the culture in which they lived: the social and cultural factors of their world provided the kindling in which the sparks of reform could spread. Based on their analysis, the reformers rejected the need for seven sacraments, retaining just two: baptism and the Lord's Supper (Holy Communion), both of which were instituted by Jesus himself.[1]

Moreover, when it came to the shape of these two sacraments, Calvin and his successors rejected both the conservatism of Martin Luther and the radicalism of Ulrich Zwingli, two earlier reformers, instead asking new questions—questions largely unimagined both by medieval Roman Catholic scholars and even by some of the reformers' Protestant colleagues. Calvin and his successors asked not, "Where is the body and blood of Jesus in relation to the bread and wine?" but

"What is the nature of the promise Jesus makes in the institution of the sacrament of Communion?" This reformulation allowed Calvin to focus on the spiritual message at the heart of Communion: God is present with us. God nourishes us. God sustains us. The reformulation also emphasized the relationship between the sacraments and the life of the body of Christ. Baptism serves as the sign and seal of our inclusion in the body of Christ: hence there is no such thing as a "private baptism." The Reformed project was innovative, energizing the tradition it received and handed on to future generations.[2]

Similar innovation characterized the Reformed approach to the offices of the church, worship, and dozens of other crucial matters facing these reformers. The forgotten hallmark of the Reformed movement, which underlies its whole history, is a particular kind of innovation—a Reformed innovation, which reflects an ability and willingness to adapt and change to new conditions, but to do so in ways that are appropriate to who we are called to be as a community of followers of Jesus Christ.

There are at least four characteristics of the leaders who engage in the kind of innovation that I'm describing: (1) the capacity to retrieve and reinterpret the rich legacy given to us as Christians; (2) a basic adaptability and flexibility that connects contemporary culture with essential matters of faith; (3) the imagination to see what is really "there" before us; and (4) the creativity to combine previously unrelated ideas to make something genuinely new.

Retrieval and Reinterpretation of Our Legacy

As we have already noted, the purpose of the Reformed movement, according to the reformers like Calvin, was not to establish a "new church" or what we have come to call a "denomination." This would have been unthinkable, anathema, to them. The purpose of the Reformation was to restore the church to its early simplicity and faithfulness of practice. In this regard they did not think they were "innovating" at all. The energy of the Reformed project in doing this is particularly well illustrated in a wonderful essay, "The Necessity of Reforming the Church," in which Calvin responds to those who were criticizing him and the other reformers. Calvin writes, "They think us right indeed in *desiring* amendment" in the church, "but not right in *attempting* it."[3]

The biblical, theological, and churchly legacy we inherited as Presbyterians is among the most extraordinary gifts handed down in the whole history of the church. But too often we dig moats and build walls and station armed guards around that legacy. Our Reformed legacy is not a castle to be defended, but a gold mine from which to draw treasure. Or, better: our legacy is a vast, rich field to be stewarded, sowed, tended, and harvested season after season.

The most Reformed question we can ask is this: What does it mean for us to be and to live as human beings created in the image of God and called to follow Jesus of Nazareth? The least Reformed question we can ask is this: What must we do to increase the market share of the Presbyterian Church to ensure the survival of our denomination? Motivation matters. An anxiety-driven church—a church motivated to attract new members just because it wants to survive—undercuts its own message. It projects a self-serving image, an image of fear, and this is simply not attractive.

When we are mindful of our legacy, however—when we remember the good news of Jesus Christ that fuels our lives and gives us hope as persons—we become forgetful of our own survival. And when we stop worrying about our survival, we, as a church, become powerfully attractive to those around us.

This paradox should come as no surprise. Jesus himself said to his first disciples: "For those who want to save their life will lose it, and those who lose their life for my sake, and for the sake of the gospel, will save it" (Mark 8:35).

The heart of our Reformed legacy, we must remember, is the Bible. The thing that has distinguished the life of faith as conceived of by the Reformed project from many other conceptions of it has been the fact that we believe (and it is a remarkable belief!) that God speaks through the Bible. Our engagement with the Bible, as Reformed Christians, has always been critical.[4] We have understood the Bible as a collection of documents assembled by human beings in actual communities of faith. We have understood the Bible as documents that reflect real limitations of knowledge and that represent a veritable catalog of the changes through which human cultures have passed for centuries. We have understood that within the Bible there is, as Karl Barth described it, "a strange world."[5] In fact, there are many strange worlds in the Bible—many different ways of being faithfully human and whole communities of faith that believe very differently from one another, but whose stories are blessed and preserved within its covers. We bear witness that God has spoken and continues to speak to us through this collection of documents. And while we certainly acknowledge that it is entirely possible to live faithfully as a Christian without sophisticated theories of interpretation, our guiding conviction has always been that a deep, critical engagement with the Bible pays enormous dividends for Christian communities. Hence we have emphasized careful, critical study and have required our ministers of the Word and Sacrament—that is, our teaching elders, our preachers and pastors—to have some grounding in the biblical languages so they can gain a deeper access to the Scriptures. Such language study helps to bridge the gap between the biblical writers and the church today—and paradoxically, to show us just how far removed from these texts we really are.

A church that still pays attention to the Bible has a better chance of being Reformed (i.e., of contributing to the Reformed project) than a church that (whether it sees itself as liberal or conservative) believes it has found another source of authority other than God's Word. There are many congregations, of course, whose members talk a great deal about their faithfulness to the Bible, but spend precious little actual time reading, studying, preaching, and hearing the Bible itself. And there are some extraordinary congregations whose members are silent about how "biblical" they are yet attend carefully and often to the reading, study, preaching, and hearing of the Bible. There is no Reformed project that is not concerned with seeing the world around us through biblical lenses.

Adaptability and Flexibility

Karl Barth once said that "theological work is distinguished from other kinds of work by the fact that anyone who desires to do it . . . [must] every day, in fact every hour, begin anew at the beginning."[6] For Barth, the beginning point for Christian God-talk (and that's what theology is) was not a principle or a commitment, but a name:

Jesus Christ. Beginning at that point, with that name, Barth called into question long-settled Christian orthodoxies and challenged the oppressive power and idolatry of Nazism.

There are many conventional hallmarks of Presbyterianism, hallmarks of doctrine and polity. But we sometimes forget that the adaptability and flexibility of the Reformed movement have never allowed any hallmark, any doctrinal standard, any idea, or any commitment to assume the place of God. Everything under heaven is subject to interrogation. The Reformed movement, from its very beginning, took it as a matter of principle that we must distinguish between what is "obsolete" (to use Calvin's own phrase) and what is vital and necessary. We must distinguish between what is a relative value (which may be a real good, but is always in competition with other values) and what is absolute and ultimate.[7]

The enduring challenge of Reformed innovation, to put it another way, is to determine what is essential and what is not essential, what we absolutely *cannot* afford to lose without losing our very souls, and what we *may* and perhaps even *must* jettison for the sake of the gospel. Calvin borrowed a term, *adiaphora,* from the ancient philosophy of Stoicism to make this distinction. That which is *adiaphora* is a matter of indifference. It is inessential. It is not worth fighting over.

As John Knox, the eventual leader of the Reformation in Scotland, discovered to his grief, Calvin took matters of indifference very seriously. Knox learned this during the years he studied and served with Calvin in Geneva, Switzerland. Shortly after being assigned by Calvin to lead a church in Germany (a church that Calvin knew well and loved), Knox split that congregation right down the middle because he bullheadedly insisted—as a matter of faith and conscience—that this church's worship must change to match his own preferences. Calvin wrote Knox a blistering letter and recalled him to Geneva.[8] Knox's zeal (which Knox felt was fully justified by the principles of Christian faith) was uncompromising, and it was unmediated by an appropriate sense of what is *adiaphora.*

By contrast, at least one legendary twentieth-century child of the Reformation, Dietrich Bonhoeffer, understood well the spirit of innovation qualified by the grace and humility reflected in knowing what is *adiaphora.* Bonhoeffer understood that when we come among a new people *we must honor the Christ who is already present among them.*[9] The flexibility and adaptability that characterizes Reformed innovation is first and foremost a spiritual reality at work in our own hearts, bending our hearts to listen humbly to others, because we know God is at work in God's world and that God may be doing things about which we have no awareness.

Imagination to See What Is Really There

The beloved curmudgeon of Christian orthodoxy, G. K. Chesterton, understood just enough about Presbyterianism to fear its excesses but not enough to embrace its genius. But Chesterton got a lot of things right about Christianity in general. One of my favorite of his insights goes like this: "We must try to recover the candour and wonder of a child; the unspoilt realism and objectivity of innocence. . . . We must invoke the most wild and soaring sort of imagination; the imagination that can see what is there."[10]

Vision is a function of imagination. As Elliot Eisner has observed in his respected study, *The Arts and the Creation of Mind,* "Imagination gives us images of the possible that provide a platform for seeing the actual." It is "by seeing the actual freshly," Eisner continues, that "we can do something about creating what lies beyond it."[11]

Such renewed, refreshed vision, such sacred imagination, is itself a function of wonder.

Perhaps the reason why some of our neighbors find Presbyterianism relatively unattractive is because our faith as Reformed Christians has ceased to surprise even us. Our neighbors yearn for mystery, and among us they find disenchantment and discord. We yawn through the parables and doze at the miracles of God among us. We have demanded that our God be no larger than our own feeble brains, then cursed the god we constructed for being so small-minded. Perhaps our lack of amazement at the gospel of Jesus Christ is only a symptom of our lack of amazement at life and creation itself. We insist that Christianity serve as an endorsement of our partisanship, our assumptions and prejudices about other people, and about society itself. We change the Magnificat of Jesus' mother (Luke 1:46–55) into a soaring anthem, while failing to hear its prophetic announcement of the reign of God. We demand that Christianity become

relevant, reducing complex theological terms into words more familiar. Thus evangelism becomes salesmanship, stewardship becomes
fundraising, and pastoral ministry becomes entrepreneurship — and
we have no clue to what has been lost in translation. We miss, along
the way, the subtlety and strange reversals of the gospel and the
claim of the reign of God that sometimes (often!) does not endorse
our ways. In the end, the relevant religion we have substituted for
Christian faith is so completely our creature as to become utterly
irrelevant, disposable along with all our other ideas because it has
become ephemeral. It does not have anything to say that we had not
already thought of ourselves.

Reformed innovation is characterized by the imagination necessary to reform what we receive, but also by a tenacious hold on that
which must not be lost.

God is up to many things in this world. Reformed innovation
reflects imagination that soars high enough to look over the walls
we have built to glimpse the wonder of a larger world, to grasp the
reverence that is the beginning of wisdom, to grab the coattails of
the justice of God's reign that lays claim to this whole created realm.

Creativity to Combine What Doesn't Ordinarily Go Together

Creativity consists in combining elements, ideas, things (all sorts of
stuff) that seem to bear no relationship to one another. The most creative minds in the history of the Christian church were able to draw
together previously disconnected ideas to create vibrant new ways to
live our faith.

- The women and men who formed those earliest Christian communities took God's age-old promise of the covenant with Israel
  and understood in the life and teachings of Jesus that this ancient
  covenant extended to the Gentiles.
- Athanasius and the Cappadocian theologians of Nicene orthodoxy
  radically reconceived the mystery of the unity of God in light of
  our encounter with God incarnate, making it necessary for us to see
  the divine as moving, engaged, and sympathetic, rather than static,
  distant, and impassible.
- The reformers revolutionized the church catholic, heralding the mes-

sage of the ancient church by using the most cutting-edge technology available, the movable-type printing press.

- Reinhold Niebuhr, Paul Tillich, Martin Luther King Jr., Gustavo Gutierrez and Desmond Tutu in the modern era, demonstrated that our ancient faith can still transform not only individual lives but whole societies: bringing moral and existentialist and linguistic philosophies; emerging political, scientific, and economic theories; and new aesthetic and ethical understandings into conversation with Christianity.
- Rebecca Chopp, Elizabeth Johnson, Sarah Coakley, Charles Taylor, and Kathryn Tanner continue today to challenge us to rethink faith's claims on cultures, and cultures' roles in understanding faith.

All of these creative minds did what they did by seeing connections others missed.

The next stage of the Reformation lies before us. It will require creativity, courage, and a sense of adventure. We will need (metaphorically speaking) to sail west in order to open a new trade route to the east, even though such an idea seems insane to the conventional mind. We will need to understand the faiths of others (in their own terms with generosity and respect) if we are to understand the faith we have been given in Jesus of Nazareth, though such an idea seems dangerous to many. We will need to ask new and bigger questions than our current answers allow if we are to move forward, though such questions are often ruled "out of bounds" by some.

All of which brings us to how we might relate the forgotten hallmark of Presbyterianism, this Reformed innovation that is the secret ingredient of the Reformed project, to our lives and faith today.

Eclipsing an Age of Anxiety with an Age of Adventure

The late Edwin Friedman, a rabbi and leading proponent of family systems theory, famously championed "adventurous leadership" as the only effective antidote to the anxiety that grips people, organizations, and institutions today. Friedman noted the apparent insanity (but actual wisdom) of the Renaissance explorers who did (in this case literally) sail west to discover a new trade route to the east.

Friedman observed that by doing this, these explorers helped medieval Europe become "unstuck" from its anxiety and conformity to convention and thus ushered in the Renaissance. In some sense, Luther and Calvin and the whole Protestant Reformation of the sixteenth century were products of the "Age of Unstuckness," the "Age of Adventure and Exploration." I suspect that the thing we most need today in our church in this profoundly anxious time is a similar spirit of adventure in leadership:

- Rather than clinging to the vestiges of Western European privilege, rather than fearing the growing influence of the two-thirds world, we would do well (especially as followers of Jesus of Nazareth) to embrace global Christianity. There is so much we can learn—not least about praising God with our whole hearts, about singing and dancing and preaching again to the deep rhythms of the gospel— from the churches of Africa, Latin America, and Asia. And there is so much we can contribute too to our sister churches, not least in the development, resourcing, and assistance in the education of their next generation of leadership. We will become a better church the more conscious we become of the global church.
- Rather than closing ourselves to interfaith communication and cooperation, we would benefit the church by learning more about the distinctive faiths of others. The more we discover about the faiths of others, the more we also discover about our own. And, ironically, the more we understand and respect the differences among us, the better able we are to appreciate our common humanity before God. The great challenge of our age may well be religious pluralism. If we do not learn to live together with respect for others and their faiths, the future looks very bleak for all of us. If we do, however, we may discover yet unimagined depths in our own reverence for God.[12]
- Rather than withering under our sense of institutional impotence and our lack of confidence in God's mission, we can entrust our church to the God who, as *The Book of Common Prayer* says, "is doing better things than we can ask or imagine."[13] Anxiety almost inevitably drives us toward Pelagianism, the ancient heresy that teaches that our salvation depends on our own efforts. There is a close analogy between the frazzled and fragmented person trying to please everyone so that he or she will be accepted and the frazzled and fragmented church desperately hoping to attract a sufficient share of the religious market to keep itself relevant (and solvent). Pelagianism is as false

as it is exhausting. If there is anything the Reformed project has consistently taught us, it is this: We cannot save ourselves. But, the good news is that we do not have to save ourselves! We have a Savior whose grace is greater than all our sin. We can entrust ourselves and our church to the God who is faithful to do that which God has promised. Faith, confidence, and courage begin with the belief that God can be trusted to accomplish God's ends. Not only are we as individual Christians "comforted" ("strengthened") because we "belong—body and soul in life and in death—to [our] faithful Savior, Jesus Christ"—but so is the church.[14]

We stand together on the brink of a new future. Of course, we *always* stand on the brink of a new future. The question is whether or not we have among us *the love, the courage, the creativity, the will*, and ultimately *the character* to meet the future's challenges, to engage in the Reformed project at this *kairos* moment in which God has placed us.

What we cannot afford to do at this moment is to allow our anxiety to drive us into "template thinking"—the kind of thinking that assumes that if a particular solution worked in a particular congregation, then it must work in every congregation. Despite our similarities of faith and history, the contextual differences among us are enormous. We need to respect these differences, and respect the faith and experience of the members of our congregations. There are faithful and wonderful congregations in this country that are experiencing significant numerical growth. There are also faithful and wonderful congregations that have declined in membership because of demographic and other factors far beyond their control.

For example, across the country there are small farm-based communities that are disappearing because of changes in the way agribusiness is conducted. Whereas a generation ago, these small communities served the needs of scores of family farms, each community having its own thriving grocery stores, pharmacies, banks, hardware stores, cafés, and often several churches, today many of these communities have virtually disappeared from the map or are in the process of doing so. Farming has gone corporate. With large companies buying up the smaller farms, the descendants of the once thriving family farms have moved to larger towns and cities to make a living. The churches that served these dwindling rural communities are disappearing, not because they have been unfaithful or unwilling to "change with the times," but because of shifts they could not have affected whatever they might have tried.

In this one example, however—an example that demonstrates what many people see as a "failure"—is a vital piece of good news for our church. When these small rural communities were first being settled a hundred or more years ago, denominations from the Reformed family of churches saw an opportunity to serve the gospel of Jesus Christ by ensuring that all of these new communities had churches in them. This is why virtually all of these small communities had congregations in them from what are sometimes derisively called the "old-line" denominations. We were the first in. Our denominations thought strategically about how to meet the challenges of forming new congregations in these emerging communities. We encouraged ministers to move west with the population. We even established seminaries to provide ministers for these communities as the population moved west. It should be no surprise to us today, then, that mainline churches are suffering disproportionate losses, and are seeing more and more struggling and closing small churches. Mainline denominations were the missional churches that generations ago established new congregations in the then-thriving small communities across the country. As these small communities are disappearing, so are the congregations in them. These churches, by and large, have not failed. They served faithfully and well for generations.

And here is some good news. The same missional vision that shaped our thinking generations ago in following the population growth westward is possible for us today. The gospel of Jesus Christ is as true today as it was in past generations, and there are more people today than there were back then. Certainly the target populations have changed in many ways, not only in physical location. Their members congregate and socialize differently. *But we can adapt to this new environment.* We can and we must prepare today's pastors and church leaders to see the opportunity that is before us, to begin new congregations where the people are and to respond to their different ways of socializing. We can and we must find new ways as Presbyterians and other Reformed Christians to support and fund the new mission enterprises necessary to reach these people.

The key will be diversification. No single approach will adequately address the challenges before us. But, if we know our history, we know that flexibility and variety have always been requisite for the church to thrive. When we look back at the story of the spread of Christian faith from the very beginning, we do not see a one-size-fits-all template. The apostles seized their opportunity to follow the Roman road system throughout an empire that was officially hostile to their enterprise. In other ages, we find the church adapting so as to nurture, sustain, and spread Christian faith, not only through local parishes, but through the establishment of a variety of religious orders, like the Benedictines, the Franciscans, and the Jesuits. Our Reformed movement was spurred on by the efforts of immigrants from various countries (including Jean Caulvin [a.k.a. John Calvin], a French émigré to Switzerland, and John Knox, a Scot who served churches in England, Switzerland, and Germany before returning home). Their witness was carried on the winds of change that swept from one European country to another. As we just noted, only a few generations ago, the Christian faith spread across this new nation as its frontier stretched westward. Today we are seeing an explosion of growth in Christianity around the globe.

There are a variety of things we can do next in our Reformed project, but, as I said earlier, whatever we do needs to reflect the fact that God is faithful to accomplish that which God promises. And, whatever we do needs to reflect who we are as God's people. Our actions need to build on our strengths — to draw from the remarkable resources we have been given.

Consequently, there are a few things we should stop doing.

First, as a church we often cite the Latin motto, *ecclesia reformata, semper reformanda*: "The church reformed, always being reformed." Note that the third word is *semper* — not *whimper*. Whimpering is neither appropriate nor helpful. A recent study found what most of us have known: the most annoying sound in the world is whining.[15] Let's take this to heart as a church! We really do need to stop whining about the losses we have suffered in numbers and prestige and influence as a mainline church. No one else cares, including (I suspect) God.

Second, we need to stop devouring ourselves in self-righteous partisanship. The old Christian song that many of us learned in camp

included the line *"They will know we are Christians by our love"* —
not *"they will know we are Christians by our self-righteous contempt
for each other."* It is really no mystery at all why a lot of people want
nothing to do with us. We need to root the spirit of schism out from
our own hearts and get on with the gospel of Jesus Christ.

Third, we need to stop running from our strengths. Surely there's
nothing wrong with the affective, emotional aspects of human nature
and faith. But there's nothing wrong with thinking about our faith
either. There's not even anything wrong with being reserved in our
worship style. One of my friends says often that she became a Presbyterian so she wouldn't have to hug people in church.

We Presbyterians have nearly stereotyped ourselves to death. We
have beaten ourselves up for being a thinking people. And it is certainly the case that contemporary North American culture does not
place a premium on thinking. But our church has been very good
at thinking about faith, and we should not abandon doing what we
are good at just because the dominant culture does not value it.
There will always be persons drawn to a church that takes serious
things seriously, a church that does not regard worship as a matter
of "styles" (whether so-called traditional worship styles or so-called
contemporary) but of substance. Even in a culture that favors bumper
sticker philosophy there will always be persons drawn to a church
that believes something of great consequence is at stake when we
speak of God. Our easily stereotyped characteristics make a contribution to the greater church and to the world that would be lost if we
simply abandoned who we are.

"Nothing is sadder than someone who has lost his memory, and
the church which has lost its memory is in the same state of senility,"
I earlier quoted Henry Chadwick as saying. And, as Simon Schama
observed: "A generation without history is a generation that not only
loses a nation's memory, but loses a sense of what it's like to be
inside a human skin."[16]

I have only hinted at what we can gain as a church by remembering and by refusing to forget who we are and what we are called to
do. The church needs the Reformed project today as much as it has
ever needed this project.

If we decide as Presbyterians to renege on our mission of participating in it, God will, I am sure, raise up others to carry on those

aspects of reformation that we historically have accomplished: emphasizing the Godness of God and the creatureliness of humanity; promoting education, scholarship, and research in everything under the sun and beyond the reaches of the known universe (including theology); and investing in the transformation of society and culture as an extension of the Christian doctrine of creation. The list goes on and on.

If others do take our place as proponents of the Reformed project, leaving us on the sidelines, they will claim our natural forebears (from John Calvin to George MacLeod) as their spiritual parents. But I don't really believe it will come to that. And I'll tell you why.

As I have traveled around the country in the past few years first as a professor, then as a dean, and now as a seminary president, I have noticed something that has surprised me. The Presbyterian Church today is healthier than at any other time in my life.

Certainly, the unprecedented growth in numbers of congregants that the church saw in the late 1940s and that peaked in 1958 is long past. But, then, in this respect mainline congregations have suffered precisely the same fate as every other North American voluntary organization that requires a considerable investment of time from those who attend local chapters. Indeed, as sociologist Robert Putnam has shown, the growth and decline in membership of mainline Protestant denominations from the early twentieth century to the present moment tracks precisely the experience of organizations such as the Parent-Teacher Associations of America.[17]

The Eisenhower Church is gone forever. The Corporate Church of the Mad Men era, with its vast national office and regional branches and layer upon layer of upper and mid-level executives is a thing of the past. But although that is the era that many of us look back to as "the rule," it was, in fact, very much "the exception." And, while there was much to celebrate in that church, there was also much not to celebrate in that church, not least its exclusion of many persons.

But as I visit congregations of all sizes and in various locations around the country, I am struck by the creative educational ventures, the vibrant worship, the lively and often profound preaching, the joyful inclusion of persons once excluded from the life of faith, and (perhaps more striking than anything else) the profound sense of mission and ministry that is occurring *in* and directly *through* congregations today. I have seen this sense of mission and ministry in a small college town in Ohio, where the congregation works closely with other congregations in Colombia and in Russia. I have witnessed it in post-Katrina New Orleans, where a historically affluent congregation has found (as they describe it) resurrection and new life by becoming a mission outpost and mission-education resource for their community and for other congregations around the nation. And I have seen it in mid-town Manhattan, where a large church that is as pluralistic and diverse in its membership as the United Nations provides ministry to homeless people, education for its community, and lively, provocative proclamation of the gospel to thousands of people on America's biggest "main street." Examples could be multiplied: churches in the Mississippi Delta and in Silicon Valley of northern California, in the hill country of central Texas and on the coast of Georgia are thriving in their own ways.

And here is what is most exciting! Churches in these diverse locations have discovered the wonder of living the *missio Dei*, God's mission in and for this world, where they are. Mission, for them, is not simply a category of a national budget carried on by proxy by someone else. Mission has become an indispensable aspect of their own lives of faith.

I remember a few years ago the painful meetings of those responsible at Presbytery and Synod levels about the future of our camps and conferences. We cared about camps and conferences because they had shaped many, if not most, of us. Some of us dated our first and sometimes our most important moments of insight and growth as young Christians to events that happened at a camp or youth conference. In those conversations, we were deeply concerned because our camps and conferences were struggling just to survive. Today there are fewer camps and conferences than there were a generation ago, and I still wish there were more. However, even while we were working hard to breathe new life into camps and conferences, something else, something new and unexpected, was growing: congregationally-sponsored mission trips. Indeed, some of us who were at that time working to resuscitate camps and conferences were ourselves designing and leading these mission trips for our youth and for other church members. We were taking youth groups and session members and deacons and others to the inner cities of America to serve in homeless shelters and summer education and recreation programs for disadvantaged children. We were taking them to Central America and into other impoverished regions of the world to build community centers and homes. Today, if we were to conduct a poll of how and where many young adults came to a deeper sense of Christian faith, a significant proportion of them would say, "It happened while I was on our church's mission trip."

The Reformed project needs, more than anything, to continue to catch up with and participate in what God is doing in the world. That is, after all, what the reformers of the sixteenth century did. We need to bring that distinctive vision we have shared from the beginning of the Reformed project to this contemporary participation. And we need to rediscover that confidence and courage that comes from remembering that the God in whom we trust is a living God still at large in this world, still inviting us to love others with the love of Jesus Christ.

What we have always done as Reformed Christians is tackle the most challenging issues of our contemporary culture with imagination and intelligence. That's what we do. We educate and provide the best scholarship possible, touching on all the great issues and problems of our time. We publish research and studies and books that the world turns to for solid and reliable knowledge and wisdom. We worship with the awareness that the worship of God *is* the purpose of the worship of God. We serve others directly by building houses and feeding starving people, certainly, *and* by attempting to affect the structures of a society that leave people homeless and hungry. We work from within our culture and society to transform it. We are not afraid of difference: in fact, we embrace and bless diversity with large and generous spirits.

If we can remember who we are and who we are called to be in Jesus Christ, the best days of the Reformed project are still ahead of us. *Ecclesia reformata, semper reformanda.*

Notes

INTRODUCTION

1. In historical terms, Reformed Christianity refers to the many denominations that trace back to the Swiss Reformed (Calvinist) stream of tradition, which began in the sixteenth century. There are hundreds of Reformed denominations worldwide. In the United States, a few of the most well-known are the Christian Reformed Church, the Reformed Church in America, the Orthodox Presbyterian Church, and the Presbyterian Church (U.S.A.).

2. Usually the phrase is given in Latin, with or without the parenthetical addition: *ecclesia reformata, semper reformanda (secundum verbi dei)*. In discussing this phrase I am indebted to Anna Case-Winters, "What do Presbyterians believe about 'Ecclesia Reformata, Semper Reformanda?' Our misused motto," in *Presbyterians Today* (May 2004). Online at http://gamc.pcusa.org/ministries/today/reformed/.

3. See Bradley Longfield, *The Presbyterian Controversy: Fundamentalists, Modernists, and Moderates* (New York: Oxford University Press, 1993).

4. Shirley C. Guthrie, *Always Being Reformed: Faith for a Fragmented World*, 2nd ed. (Louisville, KY: Westminster John Knox, 2008), xix–10. Guthrie notes that the crisis of identity versus relevance has been discussed by a number of theologians, including Karl Barth and Paul Tillich. Guthrie was specifically drawing on Jürgen Moltmann, *The Crucified God* (New York: Harper & Row, 1974).

5. A similar point is made in Case-Winters, "'Ecclesia Reformata.'"

6. Miroslav Volf, "All Due Respect," in *The Christian Century* (August 9, 2011). Online at http://periodicals.faqs.org/201108/2427611471.html. See also W. Eugene March, *The Wide, Wide Circle of Divine Love: A Biblical Case for Religious Diversity* (Louisville, KY: Westminster John Knox Press, 2005).

7. Brian K. Blount et al., "Introduction," in *True to Our Native Land: An African American New Testament Commentary*, ed. Brian K. Blount (Minneapolis: Fortress, 2007), 2.

8. John Calvin, *Institutes of the Christian Religion*, 1.6.1; ed. John T. McNeill, trans. Ford Lewis Battles, LCC (Philadelphia: Westminster Press, 1960), 1:70.

Notes 123

Notes   123

9. Cornelius Plantinga, *Engaging God's World: A Christian Vision of Faith, Learning, and Living* (Grand Rapids: Wm. B. Eerdmans, 2002), x.

10. Marion L. Soards, "Reformed Interpretation of Scripture," in *The Bible and the Churches: How Various Christians Interpret the Scriptures*, ed. Kenneth Hagen (Milwaukee: Marquette University Press, 1998), 159–74.

11. Guthrie, *Always Being Reformed*, 19–25; idem, "Rules for Biblical Interpretation in the Reformed Tradition," online: http://covnetpres.org/resources/rules-biblical-interpretation/. See also "Presbyterian Understanding and Use of Holy Scripture," and "Biblical Authority and Interpretation"; online: http://oga.pcusa.org/publications/scripture-use.pdf.

12. Dale B. Martin, *Pedagogy of the Bible: An Analysis and Proposal* (Louisville, KY: Westminster John Knox Press, 2008): 1–28.

13. In 2011, two professors at Calvin College (an institution of the Christian Reformed Church in North America) aroused strong opposition when they delivered scholarly papers questioning the traditional, literal reading of the creation accounts in Genesis in light of recent evidence about human genetics. Professor John Schneider took early retirement from the institution under pressure; Professor Daniel Harlow is still employed in 2012 but remains opposed by some. In 2010, Old Testament professor Bruce K. Waltke was dismissed from Reformed Theological Seminary for his views on evolution. Evolution has also been a flashpoint in ongoing debate over the relationship between faith and learning at Erskine College, an institution of the Associate Reformed Presbyterian Church; in March 2010 the General Synod of the denomination dismissed fourteen Board members over perceived failings. All of these events have been covered by various news outlets.

14. Becky Garrison, "Luke Johnson (*Door* Interview)," in *The Door* (March/April 1999), 14.

15. Carol Zaleski, *The Life of the World to Come* (New York: Oxford University Press, 1996). I used a similar method to explore the role of angels in biblical and Christian tradition, in Susan R. Garrett, *No Ordinary Angel: Celestial Spirits and Christian Claims about Jesus* (New Haven, CT: Yale University Press, 2008).

16. I am influenced especially by A. K. M. Adam's exposition of *differential hermeneutics* as presented in his excellent book *Faithful Interpretation: Reading the Bible in a Postmodern World* (Minneapolis: Fortress, 2006).

17. For an insightful work tracing connections between biblical interpretation and wider cultural assumptions see Ludger H. Viefhues-Bailey, *Between a Man and a Woman? Why Conservatives Oppose Same-Sex Marriage* (New York: Columbia University Press, 2010).

18. For a downloadable group study guide employing this interpretive approach see Susan R. Garrett, "Homosexuality and the Bible," available at The Thoughtful Christian.com (http://www.thethoughtfulchristian.com/Products/TC0439/the-bible-and-homosexuality.aspx).

19. See Guthrie's discussion of God's freedom from and for the world, in *Always Being Reformed*, 121–39.

20. Luke Timothy Johnson, "Imagining the World that Scripture Imagines," in *Modern Theology* 14, no. 2 (April 1998): 165–80.

CHAPTER 1: THE REFORMED PROJECT

1. "The Very Rev Professor Henry Chadwick: The Times Obituary," *The Times of London*, June 19, 2008.

2. Elizabeth Grice, "Simon Schama: Could I Have Multiple Personality Disorder?" *The Telegraph*, July 28, 2010. Online at http://www.telegraph.co.uk/culture/books/7912996/Simon-Schama-Could-I-have-multiple-personality-disorder.html.

3. The four Protestant traditions that arose in the sixteenth century are the Lutheran, Anglican, Reformed, and Radical (or Anabaptist) traditions. Brilliant charismatic leaders inspired each of these Protestant responses to the medieval Roman Catholic Church. Martin Luther's reformation is generally credited as the most influential. Luther (Lutheran), Ulrich Zwingli (Radical), and Henry VIII of England (Anglican) represent the first generation of Protestant Reformation. The Reformed movement, which began in Switzerland (and was eventually led by the Frenchman John Calvin) and which spread to the Palatinate region of Germany, Hungary, Scotland, France, and England, was part of a second wave of Reformation.

4. Roland H. Bainton, *Here I Stand: A Life of Martin Luther* (New York: New American Library, Times Mirror, 1950), 35–36.

5. Ibid., 36.

6. Carlos M. N. Eire, *War against the Idols: The Reformation of Worship from Erasmus to Calvin* (New York: Cambridge University Press, 1986), 11.

7. Ibid., 25.

8. Edward L. Cutts, *Parish Priests and Their People in the Middle Ages in England* (1898; repr., New York: AMS Press, 1970), 216.

9. A particularly helpful introduction to the practiced faith of the period can be found in Diarmaid MacCulloch, *The Reformation: A History* (New York: Viking/Penguin, 2004), 3–52.

10. E. Harris Harbison, *The Christian Scholar in the Age of the Reformation* (New York: Charles Scribner's Sons, 1956), 100–101.

11. Raymond A. Mentzer, "The Piety of Townspeople and City Folk," in *A People's History of Christianity*, vol. 5, *Reformation Christianity*, ed. Peter Matheson (Minneapolis: Fortress Press, 2007), 23.

12. Eire notes, for example, that "magic is an awesome and frightful thing," providing "some assurance of control over fate," but also making "one depend upon fickle and unpredictable powers." "Religious anxiety must have increased proportionately," he reasons, "to the distancing of God through materialism and 'parapolytheism.'" *War against the Idols*, 25.

13. Ibid., 317.

14. Eire sees the humanist (and the subsequent Reformed) critique of medieval superstition, magical thinking, and corruption as inspired primarily by Platonic and neo-Platonic thought (see Eire, 28–53, 197–233, 311–13). But this interpretation does not adequately take into account the fact that medieval

Catholicism was thoroughly suffused with essentially this worldview, so much so that intellectual historians such as Isaiah Berlin have referred to this way of thinking that dominated Western civilization for some two thousand years simply as the *philosophia perennis*, i.e., the perennial philosophy. It was this worldview, incidentally, which bequeathed to us both the philosophical idealism that forces us to separate matter from spirit and the historical idealism that resulted in the catastrophic development of scores of utopian dreams, which almost inevitably ended in dystopian nightmares. It also gave us that worldview that has contributed so much to religious exclusivism, the assumption that for every real question there can be one and only one right answer. See Isaiah Berlin, *The Crooked Timber of Humanity: Chapters in the History of Ideas,* ed. Henry Hardy (New York: Vintage edition, 1992), 1–48, 70–90.

15. Bainton, *Here I Stand,* 58.

16. Ibid., 60.

17. Eamon Duffy, *Saints and Sinners: A History of the Popes* (New Haven, CT: Yale University Press, 1997; London: The Folio Society, 2009), 214.

18. Ibid.

19. J. Kelley Sowards, "Introduction," in *The* Julius Exclusus *of Erasmus,* trans. Paul Pascal (Bloomington: Indiana University Press, 1968), 7.

20. Peter Matheson, "Reforming from Below," *Reformation Christianity,* 8.

21. John Calvin, "Reply to Sadoleto," in *Calvin: Theological Treatises,* ed. J. K. S. Reid (Philadelphia: Westminster, 1954), 221–56.

22. C. S. Lewis, *Mere Christianity* (New York: Macmillan, 1952), v–xii.

23. James Mackinnon, *Calvin and the Reformation* (London: Longman, Green and Co., 1936), 293.

24. Karl Barth, *Church Dogmatics,* I/1, 2nd ed., eds. G. W. Bromiley and T. F. Torrance (Edinburgh: T. & T. Clark, 1975), 112.

25. Eberhard Jüngel, *Karl Barth: A Theological Legacy,* trans. Garrett E. Paul (Philadelphia: Westminster, 1986), 27.

26. Eberhard Busch, *Karl Barth: His Life from Letters and Autobiographical Texts,* trans. John Bowden (Philadelphia: Fortress, 1976), 496.

27. Eberhard Busch quoting Karl Barth in Busch, *Karl Barth,* 417.

28. The Theological Declaration of Barmen, 8.11.

CHAPTER 2: WHAT'S NEXT FOR THE REFORMED PROJECT?

1. Dietrich Bonhoeffer, *Dietrich Bonhoeffer Works,* vol. 12, *Berlin: 1932–1933,* trans. Isabel Best and David Higgins, ed. Larry L. Rasmussen (Minneapolis: Fortress, 2009).

2. Ibid., 300.

3. Ibid., 305.

4. Ernst Käsemann, *Perspectives on Paul* (Philadelphia: Fortress, 1971), 120–21.

5. Matthew Myer Boulton, *God against Religion: Rethinking Christian Theology through Worship* (Grand Rapids: Eerdmans, 2008), xv–xviii, 1–20, 161–94.

6. This concept of "wholly-otherness" is frequently attributed to Karl Barth, particularly to his commentary on the Epistle to the Romans. The concept actually, as Barth acknowledges, comes from Søren Kierkegaard, who protested the way in which the official state religion of Denmark had co-opted Christianity's rites and messages for its own ends.

7. John T. McNeill, "Osiander, Andreas," in *A Dictionary of Christian Theology,* ed. Allan Richardson (Philadelphia: Westminster, 1969), 249.

8. John Calvin, *Institutes of the Christian Religion,* 3.6.5–12.

9. Phil. 2:5–6 NEB.

10. For example, Mark 7:1–23 and Matt. 12:1–14.

11. The "infinite qualitative difference" between God and humanity was posited by Søren Kierkegaard and constituted a key element in the theology of Karl Barth.

12. John Calvin, *Commentary on Galatians, Ephesians, Philippians and Colossians,* eds. David W. Torrance and Thomas F. Torrance, trans. T. H. L. Parker (Edinburgh: Oliver and Boyd, 1965), 136 (from the commentary on Ephesians).

13. Lesslie Newbigin, *Foolishness to the Greeks: The Gospel and Western Culture* (London: SPCK, 1986), 127.

14. George MacLeod, *Only One Way Left* (Glasgow: Iona Community, 1953), 37. The Iona community is an ecumenical community founded by MacLeod in 1938, with activities centered on the island of Iona. It was originally under the jurisdiction of the Church of Scotland.

15. Ibid., 38.

16. Emil Brunner, *Dogmatics,* vol. 3, *The Christian Doctrine of the Church, Faith, and the Consummation,* trans. David Cairns and T. H. L. Parker (Philadelphia: Westminster, 1960), 29; Kathryn Tanner, *Theories of Culture: A New Agenda for Theology* (Minneapolis: Fortress, 1997), 93ff.

17. Alan E. Lewis, "Unmasking Idolatries: Vocation in the *Ecclesia Crucis,*" in *Incarnational Ministry: The Presence of Christ in Church, Society, and Family,* ed. Christian D. Kettler and Todd H. Speidell (Colorado Springs: Helmers & Howard, 1990), 113.

CHAPTER 3: WHY A THINKING FAITH STILL MATTERS

1. Nicholas D. Kristof, "Believe It, Or Not," *The New York Times,* Friday, August 15, 2003, A29. Online at http://www.nytimes.com/2003/08/15/opinion/believe-it-or-not.html.

2. For discussion of the life of the mind as the service of God see John Leith, *The Reformed Imperative: What the Church Has to Say That No One Else Can Say* (Philadelphia: Westminster, 1988), 14–15, 22–24.

3. Arthur M. Schlesinger Jr., *The Age of Jackson* (Boston: Little, Brown and Company), xv–xxxii, 3–44.

4. Hugh Heclo (*On Thinking Institutionally* [Boulder: Paradigm Publishers, 2008], 1–43) charts the history of anti-institutionalism and its implications.

5. David Brooks, "The Tea Party Teens," *The New York Times,* January 5, 2010, A17. Online at http://www.nytimes.com/2010/01/05/opinion/05brooks.html.

6. Tom Long, "A Matter of Depth," sermon preached at Trinity Presbyterian Church, Atlanta, Georgia, Sunday, October 5, 2003.

7. Christopher Hitchens, *God Is Not Great: How Religion Poisons Everything* (New York: Twelve, 2007); Richard Dawkins, *The God Delusion* (Boston: Houghton Mifflin, 2006).

8. Craig Dykstra, "Thinking Faith: A Theological Education for the American Churches," *Living Light* 27, no. 1 (1990): 7–16.

9. Reinhold Niebuhr, *The Irony of American History* (New York: Charles Scribner's Sons, 1952), 169.

10. The line ascribed to Tertullian (and often cited) derives from *De Carne Christi* 5.4; see http://en.wikiquote.org/wiki/Tertullian. For Campbell's remark, see Will D. Campbell, *Brother to a Dragonfly* (New York: Seabury Press, 1977), 220; see also http://theviewfromthisseat.blogspot.com/2010/07/were-all-bastards.html.

11. Niebuhr, *Irony*, 170.

12. For example, by those who represent the so-called New Calvinism or the self-proclaimed "tough-minded Christianity." On the latter group, see William Dembski and Thomas Schirrmacher, eds., *Tough-Minded Christianity* (Nashville: B&H Publishing Group, 2008).

13. Reinhold Niebuhr, *The Nature and Destiny of Man: A Christian Interpretation,* vol. 1, *Human Nature* (New York: Charles Scribner's Sons, 1941), 2–3.

14. On the point of interest in self-transcendence and reverence, see Paul Woodruff, *Reverence: Renewing a Forgotten Virtue* (New York: Oxford University Press, 2001); and Karen Armstrong, *The Spiral Staircase: My Climb out of Darkness* (New York: Anchor Books, 2004). Related to the issue of young adults asking "big questions," see W. Robert Connor, "The Right Time and Place for Big Questions," *Chronicle of Higher Education,* June 9, 2006, B8.

15. Alistair Moffat, *The Wall: Rome's Greatest Frontier* (Edinburgh: Birlinn Ltd., 2009), 37.

16. Loren Mead, *The Once and Future Church: Reinventing the Congregation for a New Mission Frontier* (Washington D.C.: Alban Institute, 1991), 4–9.

17. Edwin Friedman, the most persuasive proponent for "adventurous leadership" in the face of what he called "the chronic anxiety that characterizes the emotional processes of contemporary American civilization," developed these ideas most fully in his posthumously published *A Failure of Nerve: Leadership in the Age of the Quick Fix,* eds. Margaret M. Treadwell and Edward W. Beal (New York: Seabury Books, 1999/2007); see esp. 29–50.

18. Garry Wills, *Certain Trumpets: The Call of Leaders* (New York: Simon & Schuster, 1994), 21.

19. Michael Jinkins, "Thinking Out Loud." Online: http://www.michaeljinkins.blogspot.com/.

20. Cornel West, *Race Matters* (Boston: Beacon Press, 2001); idem, *Democracy Matters: Winning the Fight against Imperialism* (New York: Penguin Press, 2004).

21. Marilynne Robinson, *Gilead* (New York: Farrar, Straus and Giroux, 2004); idem, *Home* (New York: Farrar, Straus and Giroux, 2008); idem, *The Death of Adam: Essays on Modern Thought* (New York: Picador, 2005).

22. Stephen R. Prothero, *Religious Literacy: What Every American Needs to Know—and Doesn't* (San Francisco: HarperSanFrancisco, 2007); idem, *God Is Not One: The Eight Rival Religions That Run the World—and Why Their Differences Matter* (New York: HarperOne, 2010).

CHAPTER 4: SCHISM, THE UNINTENDED CONSEQUENCE OF THE REFORMED PROJECT

1. Calvin's "The Necessity of Reforming the Church" appears in J. K. S. Reid, ed., *Calvin: Theological Treatises* (Philadelphia: Westminster Press, 1954), 183–216; Calvin wrote it at Bucer's request for the Diet of Spires which was called for in February 1544. The "Prefatory Address to King Francis I of France," one of the most frequently cited of Calvin's writings, opens his *Institutes of the Christian Religion* (ed. John T. McNeill; trans. Ford Lewis Battles [Philadelphia: The Westminster Press, 1960], 1:9–31).

2. David H. Kelsey, *To Understand God Truly* (Louisville, KY: Westminster/ John Knox Press, 1992), 32. Kelsey is here borrowing from G. K. Chesterton.

3. Biblical scholars have explored "Paul's unfolding theology of inclusivity"; see Eung Chun Park, *Either Jew or Gentile: Paul's Unfolding Theology of Inclusivity* (Louisville, KY: Westminster John Knox Press, 2003). Note particularly the introduction (pp. 1–8), and chapter 6, titled "Paul's Efforts for the Unity of the Church" (pp. 65–73).

4. Everett Ferguson, ed., *Doctrinal Diversity: Varieties of Early Christianity* (New York and London: Garland Publishing, 1999). The editorial introduction provides a helpful overview of the history of diversity in the early church. Andrew Louth's essay, "Unity and Diversity in the Church of the Fourth Century," 1–17, is particularly enlightening.

5. Kathryn Tanner, *Theories of Culture: A New Agenda for Theology* (Minneapolis: Fortress, 1997), 124; see also 124–55.

6. Michael Jinkins, *Christianity, Tolerance and Pluralism: A Theological Engagement with Isaiah Berlin's Social Theory* (London: Routledge, 2004), 7–8.

7. *The Oxford Dictionary of the Christian Church* (eds. F. L. Cross and E. A. Livingstone; 3rd ed. [Oxford/New York: Oxford University Press, 1997], 1462) is typical in its definition of the term.

8. J. G. Davies, "Schism," in Alan Richardson, ed., *A Dictionary of Christian Theology* (Philadelphia: Westminster, 1969), 305.

9. Ibid.

10. Ibid.

11. Ibid., 305–6.

12. Ibid., 306.

13. John Calvin, *Calvin's New Testament Commentaries, A New Translation*, eds. David W. Torrance and Thomas F. Torrance, vol. 9, *The First Epistle of Paul to the Corinthians*, trans. John W. Fraser (Grand Rapids, Eerdmans, 1960), 238.

14. Ibid., 237.

15. Ibid., 239.

16. John Calvin, *Selected Works of John Calvin: Tracts and Letters*, eds. Henry Beveridge and Jules Bonnet, vol. 6, *Letters, Part 3, 1554–1558* (Grand Rapids: Baker, 1983), 117–19 (Letter CCCLXXX) and 189–91 (Letter CCCCIV).

17. T. H. L. Parker, *John Calvin: A Biography* (Louisville, KY: Westminster John Knox Press, 2007), 165.

18. Calvin, *Institutes of the Christian Religion*, 4.1.2; italics mine.

19. Parker, *Calvin*, 166. Italics mine.

20. Ibid., 167.

21. Calvin, *Institutes*, 4.2.6.

22. François Wendel, *Calvin: The Origins and Development of his Religious Thought*, trans. Philip Mairet (New York: Harper & Row, Publishers, 1950), 297–98.

23. David Johnson, personal correspondence, September 2, 2008.

24. Calvin, *Institutes*, 4.1.2; see footnote 6, and see also *Institutes* 4.2.1. The Second Helvetic Confession states: "The Church has always existed and it will always exist."

25. Ibid., 4.2.12.

26. Ibid.

27. Ibid.

28. One wishes that Calvin's successors had been as resistant to retrenchment as some later Calvin scholars have been. The point is well-illustrated in R. T. Kendall's superb survey, *Calvin and English Calvinism to 1649* (Oxford: Oxford University Press, 1979).

29. William J. Bouwsma's contribution, for example, looks primarily at Calvin (*John Calvin: A Sixteenth Century Portrait* [Oxford/New York: Oxford University Press, 1988]), while some other historical studies inquire more broadly into the Reformation and its aftermath: see, for example, Diarmaid MacCulloch, *The Reformation* (London/New York: Penguin Books, 2003); Carter Lindberg, *The European Reformations* (Oxford: Blackwell Publishers, Ltd., 1996); and Margo Todd, *The Culture of Protestantism in Early Modern Scotland* (New Haven, CT: Yale University Press, 2002).

30. James Simpson, *Burning to Read: English Fundamentalism and its Reformation Opponents* (Cambridge, MA: Harvard University Press, 2007), 142–83.

31. I explore more fully the significance of tradition and betrayal in my examination of the concept of *paradidōmi* in "De-scribing Church: Ecclesiology in Semiotic Dialogue," in *The Church Faces Death* (New York/Oxford: Oxford University Press, 1999), 33–49.

32. The research associated with Bellah's name traces the larger social implications of a particular kind of individualism that inevitably erodes "the good society" (Robert N. Bellah, Richard Madsen, William M. Sullivan, Ann Swidler, and Steven M. Tipton, *Habits of the Heart: Individualism and Commitment in American Life* [Berkeley: University of California Press, 1985]; see also their remarkable sequel, *The Good Society* [New York: Alfred A. Knopf, 1991]; and,

more recently, Robert D. Putnam, *Bowling Alone: The Collapse and Revival of American Community* [New York: Simon & Schuster, 2000]).

33. John Calvin, *The Epistles of Paul the Apostle to the Galatians, Ephesians, Philippians and Colossians*, trans. T. H. L. Parker, *Calvin's New Testament Commentaries*, vol. 11 (Grand Rapids: Eerdmans, 1965), 298.

34. Ibid., 136. Also, see Calvin's use of the "mirror" analogy in *Institutes*, 3.24.5, where Calvin writes, "But if we have been chosen in him, we shall not find assurance of our election in ourselves; and not even in God the Father, if we conceive him as severed from his Son. Christ, then, is the mirror wherein we must, and without self-deception may, contemplate our own election."

35. Trevor Hart, "Humankind in Christ and Christ in Humankind: Salvation as Participation in our Substitute in the Theology of John Calvin," *Scottish Journal of Theology* 42, no. 1 (1989): 79.

36. Ernst Käsemann, *Perspectives on Paul* (Philadelphia: Fortress 1971),120–21.

37. Karl Barth, *Church Dogmatics*, II/2, *The Doctrine of God*, trans. G. W. Bromiley, et al. (Edinburgh: T. & T. Clark, 1978), 94–145; also Karl Barth, *Church Dogmatics*, IV/1, *The Doctrine of Reconciliation*, trans. G. W. Bromiley (Edinburgh: T. & T. Clark, 1980), 22–78 (note particularly 34–49). (*Church Dogmatics* hereafter cited as *CD*.)

38. Karl Barth, *CD* II/2:111

39. Ibid.

40. See, for example, Calvin's Commentary on Hebrews 6–10 (John Calvin, *Hebrews and I and II Peter*, eds. David W. Torrance and Thomas F. Torrance, trans. W. B. Johnston, Calvin's New Testament Commentaries [Grand Rapids: Wm. B. Eerdmans, 1963], 71–156).

CHAPTER 5: WONDER, SPIRITUAL TRANSFORMATION, AND REFORMED WORSHIP

1. Donald E. Miller, *Reinventing American Protestantism: Christianity in the New Millennium* (Berkeley: University of California Press, 1997), 3.

2. Problems in Miller's book pertain to its weak ecclesiology, the insufficiency of attention given to historical antecedents of the so-called new paradigm churches, lack of awareness of culturally determined aspects of informal worship, and the significance of the ministries of Sacrament and Word in the mediation of the sacred.

3. Ibid.

4. William F. Arndt and F. Wilbur Gingrich, *A Greek-English Lexicon of the New Testament and Other Early Christian Literature* (Chicago: University of Chicago Press, 1957), 513.

5. We see, for example, how, in the early Christian hymn quoted in Phil. 2:5–11, Christ is described as being "in the *form* of God" and "taking the *form* of a slave [or servant]." In both cases the word *form* translates the Greek *morphē*, which indicates one's essential character or attributes made visible. Over-against this visible form of the essential attributes (*morphē*) in vv. 6–7, the author of the hymn contrasts "being found in human *appearance*" (*schēmati*) in v. 8 (v. 7c in some translations).

6. Krister Stendahl, *Final Account: Paul's Letter to the Romans* (Minneapolis: Fortress Press, 1995), 46.

7. Miller, *Reinventing American Protestantism*, 3.

8. Jonathan Edwards's *Treatise Concerning the Religious Affections* (1746) remains the definitive source for understanding this event. See also Amy Schrager Lang, "A Flood of Errors: Chauncy and Edwards in the Great Awakening," in Nathan O. Hatch and Harry S. Stout, eds., *Jonathan Edwards and the American Experience* (New York: Oxford University Press, 1988), 160–73; and Michael Jinkins, "The 'True Remedy': Jonathan Edwards' Soteriological Perspective as Observed in his Revival Treatises," *Scottish Journal of Theology*, 48, no. 2 (1995):185–209. Also note Bradley J. Longfield, *The Presbyterian Controversy: Fundamentalists, Modernists, and Moderates* (New York: Oxford University Press, 1991) for a careful study of the Presbyterian schism in the early twentieth century; and Robert William Fogel, *The Fourth Great Awakening and the Future of Egalitarianism* (Chicago: University of Chicago Press, 2000), for a sweeping analysis of the various "spiritual revivals" that have periodically emerged in American society, and the political and social changes attending them.

9. Susan R. Garrett reflects on the ways in which Paul, though himself a spiritual mystic, insisted on order in the worship of the early Christian communities. "Proper ordering of worship is, in Paul's view, yet one more way of expressing divine love, which is the mark of God's own Spirit in our lives." See Susan R. Garrett, *No Ordinary Angel: Celestial Spirits and Christian Claims about Jesus* (New Haven, CT: Yale University Press, 2008), 71.

10. Ibid., 69–73.

11. Ibid., 69.

12. Ibid.

13. Ibid., 70.

14. Seward Hiltner, *Preface to Pastoral Theology: The Ministry and Theory of Shepherding* (Nashville: Abingdon Press, 1958).

15. Ibid., 56.

16. Ibid., 19.

17. Ibid., 61.

18. From Gregory of Nazianzus, John Chrysostom, and Gregory the Great, to Richard Baxter, George Herbert, Charles Haddon Spurgeon, and Reinhold Niebuhr, these three perspectives, communicating, organizing, and shepherding, have historically informed, grounded and corrected the various practices of pastoral ministry.

19. David L. Bartlett, *Ministry in the New Testament* (Minneapolis: Fortress Press, 1993); Donald E. Messer, *Contemporary Images of Christian Ministry* (Nashville: Abingdon Press, 1989); Avery Dulles, *Models of the Church* (New York: Doubleday, expanded edition 1987). Even relatively unbalanced attempts to define pastoral ministry, for example, as an executive office, as in the common misinterpretation of H. Richard Niebuhr's description of the pastor as "pastoral director" (*The Purpose of the Church and Its Ministry* [New York: Harper & Row, 1956], 76–81); or as a kind of anti-executive office, as in Henri J. M. Nouwen's

knowingly idealistic vision of church leadership (in *The Name of Jesus: Reflections on Christian Leadership* [New York: Crossroad, 1994], 9–28) draw on the same perspectives for support and critique of their models. Jackson Carroll (in "Facing the Giants: Pastoral Leadership in a Time of Change," an address presented at a conference on "Resources for the Journey of Pastoral Ministry," Austin Presbyterian Seminary, February 27, 2002, 14–15) observes that Niebuhr

> attempted . . . a re-theologizing of the minister's role. Like [Samuel] Blizzard, Niebuhr saw a considerable disjunction between what ministers were actually doing in congregations—their increasing managerial responsibilities as heads of growing suburban congregations—and the conception they had of their pastoral office. As a remedy, he proposed recovering the image of "pastoral director" as a way of giving ministers a more adequate concept of their office. The image was drawn from the abbot's role in the Benedictine tradition as the one responsible for maintaining the community's health. Niebuhr believed that this image, normatively interpreted, would give pastors a theological conception of their office appropriate to the new context in which they worked. To be sure, they could continue to preach, lead in worship, teach, and give pastoral care. But they would also understand that administrative tasks, far from being necessary evil to be endured, are essential for building and shaping a congregation's community and helping it engage in its mission of increasing the love of God and neighbor. Unfortunately, the normative meaning of Niebuhr's image was never fully understood or appreciated, and he was sharply criticized for proposing an a-theological, "big-operator" view of ministry.

20. Hiltner, *Preface to Pastoral Theology*, 58. This fourth perspective is the originating cause or perspective that is fundamental to and that has the power to reorient Hiltner's perspectives of communicating, organizing and shepherding through the various practices of pastoral ministry.

21. I am reminded by a comment by a pastor several years ago in a focus group I was conducting. He said that the only courses he took in seminary that had remained relevant were those that helped him better understand the Bible, the theological legacies of his faith tradition, the meaning of worship, and the history of the church. All of the courses touted as "relevant" in his seminary were out-of-date within three years of graduation.

22. John T. McNeill, ed., *John Calvin on God and Political Duty* (Indianapolis: The Bobbs-Merrill Company, Inc., second, revised edition, 1956), vii. McNeill comments further: "Throughout his writings Calvin stresses his unwavering belief that the high Sovereign of the universe is also intimately present in the world of mankind. He sees God's hand in all historical events, and never doubts that in our personal affairs and choices we have 'dealings with God' all the days of our life."

23. Gerard Manley Hopkins, "God's Grandeur." Quoted in Ralph Harper, *On Presence* (Baltimore: Johns Hopkins University Press, 1991), 77.

24. Johanna W. H. van Wijk-Bos, *Reimagining God: The Case for Scriptural Diversity* (Louisville, KY: Westminster John Knox, 1995), 31.

25. Ibid., 32.

26. Note Friedrich Heiler, *Prayer: A Study in the History and Psychology of Religion* (Oxford: Oxford University Press, 1932), particularly the chapter "Prayer in Prophetic Religion," 227–85.

27. Rudolf Otto, *The Idea of the Holy: An Inquiry into the Non-rational Factor in the Idea of the Divine and Its Relation to the Rational* (New York: Oxford University Press, 1958 [first published 1923]), 76–77.

28. Rudolf Otto, *Religious Essays: A Supplement to the Idea of the Holy* (London: Oxford University Press, 1931), vi.

29. See Isaiah Berlin, *Three Critics of the Enlightenment: Vico, Hamann, Herder*, ed. Henry Hardy (London: Pimlico Press, 2000), 280–312.

30. Otto, *The Idea of the Holy*, 83.

31. Ibid., 85.

32. Søren Kierkegaard, *Fear and Trembling*, edited and translated by Howard V. Hong and Edna H. Hong (Princeton: Princeton University Press, 1983), passim.

33. William James, *The Varieties of Religious Experience: A Study in Human Nature: Being the Gifford Lectures on Natural Religion Delivered at Edinburgh in 1901–1902* (New York: The Modern Library edition, 1994), 210–84.

34. Karl Barth, *Church Dogmatics* I/1, eds. G. W. Bromiley and T. F. Torrance (Edinburgh: T. & T. Clark, 1975), 322. Herein lies the crucial paradox of God's holiness and the secularity of God's world: The closer God draws to us, the more clearly we discern that we are creatures and that God alone is Creator. It is the immanence of the holy God that convinces us that there is between God and us an infinite qualitative difference.

35. Rudolf Otto, *The Idea of the Holy*, 12–13.

36. Ibid., 31–49. The phrase, "intuition of our ultimate dependence on God" comes from the early nineteenth century Reformed theologian, Friedrich Schleiermacher. The proper sense of one's self in the presence of the holy, according to Schleiermacher, can be termed an "immediate feeling," an "intuition," or "sense" of one's "ultimate dependence upon God." Schleiermacher makes apparent, in his explication of "God-consciousness," more than anywhere else, his continuity with the Reformed project begun in Calvin. See Friedrich Schleiermacher, *The Christian Faith*, eds. H. R. Mackintosh and J. S. Steward (Edinburgh: T. & T. Clark, 1928), 3–31, 131–56. Whatever else one may say about Calvin's "knowledge of God," it is grounded in an "existential apprehension," which senses one's utter helplessness, one's *creatureliness*, in the presence of the holy God. See John Calvin, *Institutes of the Christian Religion* 1.1.1, ed. John T. McNeill, trans. Ford Lewis Battles (Philadelphia: Westminster Press, 1960), 1:35–36; see editorial footnotes. Otto's understanding of the human response to the sacred is consistent with both Calvin and Schleiermacher when he says that, in the presence of the holy, we are overwhelmed by our "creature-consciousness," and we are undone by that consciousness of ourselves in relationship to the holy, the numinous, who dismantles our pretensions, our pride and notions of independence and power. See Otto, *The Idea of the Holy*, 10–11.

37. Jonathan Edwards, *Religious Affections*, ed. John E. Smith (New Haven, CT: Yale University Press, 1959), 263.

38. Abraham Heschel, *Man Is Not Alone: A Philosophy of Religion* (New York: Farrar, Straus and Giroux, 1951), 282–84.

39. Frederick Buechner's novel *Godric* is based on this real hermit who is buried in a monastery near Durham.

40. Otto, *The Idea of the Holy*, 60.

41. Karl Barth, *The Word of God and the Word of Man*, trans. Douglas Horton (Gloucester: Peter Smith, 1978 edition [originally published 1928]), 108–9.

42. Richard Lischer, *Open Secrets: A Spiritual Journey through a Country Church* (New York: Doubleday, 2001), 232.

CHAPTER 6: THEOLOGICAL EDUCATION AND THE REFORMED PROJECT

1. Karl Jaspers, *The Origin and Goal of History* (New Haven, CT: Yale University Press, 1953), 1–4.

2. Ibid., 2–4.

3. James Davison Hunter, *To Change the World: The Irony, Tragedy, and Possibility of Christianity in the Late Modern World* (New York: Oxford University Press, 2010); Kathryn Tanner, *Theories of Culture: A New Agenda for Theology* (Minneapolis: Fortress, 1997); Robert William Fogel, *The Fourth Great Awakening and the Future of Egalitarianism* (Chicago: University of Chicago Press, 2000).

4. Daniel O. Aleshire, *Earthen Vessels: Hopeful Reflections on the Work and Future of Theological Schools* (Grand Rapids: Eerdmans, 2008), 129.

5. Dorothy C. Bass and Craig Dykstra, *For Life Abundant: Practical Theology, Theological Education, and Christian Ministry* (Grand Rapids: Eerdmans, 2008), 11.

6. Lizette Alvarez, "Koran-Burning Pastor Unrepentant in Face of Furor," *The New York Times*, April 2, 2011.

7. Arnold B. Rhodes, *The Mighty Acts of God*, ed. W. Eugene March, rev. ed. (Louisville: Geneva Press, 2000).

8. Lillian Daniel and Martin B. Copenhaver, *This Odd and Wondrous Calling: The Public and Private Lives of Two Ministers* (Grand Rapids: Eerdmans, 2009), 16.

9. Clarence Jordan, *The Substance of Faith*, ed. Dallas Lee (New York: Association Press, 1972), 42.

10. José Míguez-Bonino, *Room to Be People*, trans. Vicky Leach (Philadelphia: Fortress, 1975), 9–10.

11. Marcus Borg, *Meeting Jesus Again for the First Time: The Historical Jesus and the Heart of Contemporary Faith* (San Francisco: HarperSanFrancisco, 1990).

12. Rowan Williams, *On Christian Theology* (Oxford: Blackwell, 2000), xiii–xv.

13. W. Robert Connor, "The Right Time and Place for Big Questions," *Chronicle of Higher Education*, June 9, 2006, B8.

14. Thomas Merton, *New Seeds of Contemplation* (New York: New Directions, 2007), 3.

15. The annual Kentuckiana Metroversity Awards for Outstanding Instructional Development are made possible by a grant given by H. Charles Grawemeyer and from Metroversity Funds.

16. Burton Z. Cooper, *Why, God?* (Atlanta: John Knox Press, 1988).

CHAPTER 7: A FORGOTTEN HALLMARK OF THE REFORMED PROJECT

1. T. H. L. Parker, *John Calvin: A Biography* (Louisville, KY: Westminster John Knox Press, 2007), 68; and Wilhelm Niesel, *The Theology of Calvin* (Philadelphia: Westminster Press, 1956), 215–22.

2. See the discussion of Paul's use of the term *paredōka* ("I handed on") in 1 Cor. 15:1–3a, in Michael Jinkins, *The Church Faces Death: Ecclesiology in a Post-Modern Context* (New York: Oxford University Press, 1999), 40.

3. John Calvin, *The Necessity of Reforming the Church,* ed. J. K. S. Reid (Philadelphia: Westminster Press, 1954), 185.

4. See Marion L. Soards, "Reformed Interpretation of Scripture," in *The Bible in the Churches: How Various Christians Interpret the Scriptures,* ed. Kenneth Hagen (Milwaukee: Marquette University Press, 1998), 159–74.

5. Karl Barth, *The Word of God and the Word of Man* (Gloucester: Peter Smith, 1978), 28–50.

6. Eberhard Jüngel, *Karl Barth: A Theological Legacy,* trans. Garrett E. Paul (Philadelphia: Westminster Press, 1986), 18–19.

7. Calvin, *The Necessity of Reforming the Church,* 185–91; and John Calvin, "Reply to Sadoleto," in *Calvin: Theological Treatises,* ed. J. K. S. Reid (Philadelphia: Westminster 1954), 229–31.

8. Letter to John Knox, in John Calvin, *Selected Works of John Calvin,* eds. Henry Beveridge and Jules Bonnet, 7 vols. (Grand Rapids: Baker Book House, 1983), 6:189–91.

9. Dietrich Bonhoeffer, *Christ the Center* (New York: Harper & Row, 1966), 59–61.

10. G. K. Chesterton, *The Everlasting Man* (London: Hodder & Stoughton, 1925), 9.

11. Elliott W. Eisner, *The Arts and the Creation of Mind* (New Haven, CT: Yale University Press, 2002), 4.

12. Paul Woodruff, *Reverence: Renewing a Forgotten Virtue* (New York: Oxford University Press, 2002).

13. Appropriately, *The Book of Common Prayer* places this phrase in a prayer "for those we love."

14. See the first question of the Heidelberg Catechism.

15. Rosemarie Sokol Chang and Nicholas S. Thompson, "Whines, Cries, and Motherese: Their Relative Power to Distract," *Journal of Social, Evolutionary, and Cultural Psychology* 5, no. 2 (2011): 10–20.

16. The oft-quoted statement by Henry Chadwick was included in his obituary in *The Times of London,* June 19, 2008. The statement by Simon Schama may be found

in Elizabeth Grice, "Simon Schama: Could I Have Multiple Personality Disorder?" *The Telegraph*, July 28, 2010. Online at http://www.telegraph.co.uk/culture/books/7912996/Simon-Schama-Could-I-have-multiple-personality-disorder.html.

17. Robert Putnam, *Bowling Alone: The Collapse and Revival of American Community* (New York: Simon & Schuster, 2001). See also Robert Putnam and David E. Campbell, *American Grace: How Religion Divides and Unites Us* (New York: Simon & Schuster, 2010).

CPSIA information can be obtained at www.ICGtesting.com
Printed in the USA
LVOW130058010912

296909LV00002BA/1/P

9 780664 238438